To Brian & Jeremy,
Some bits may
be of interest.

Gerard

2

"I didn't know that..."
[*Musings to share with my Aughrim friends.*]

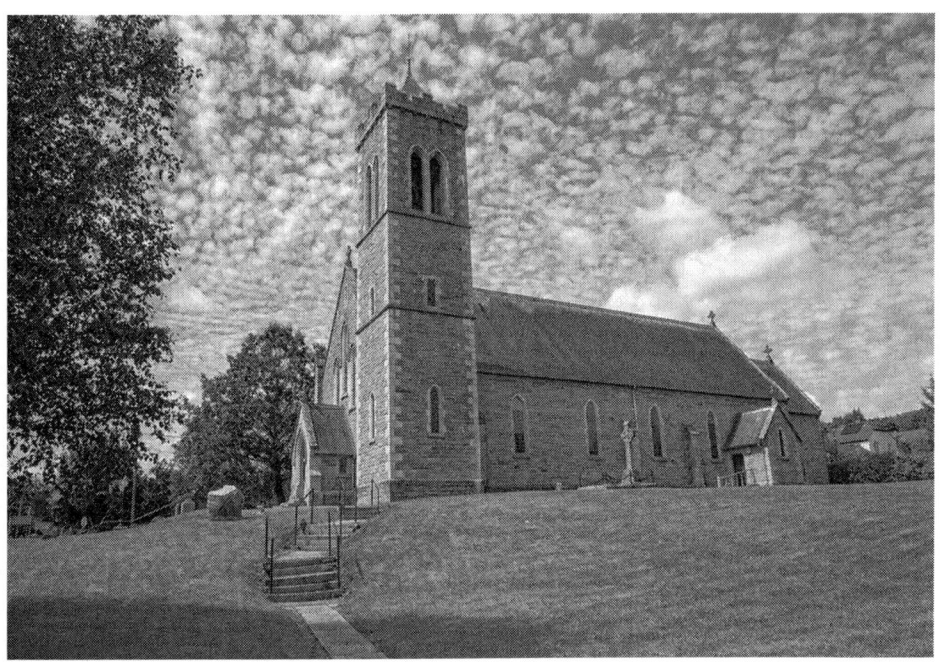

© Gearoid Griffin 2024

All rights reserved. No part of this publication may be reproduced, stored in a retrieval system or transmitted in any form or by any means, electronic, mechanical, photocopying, recording or otherwise without the prior written permission of the publisher.
This book is sold subject to the condition that it shall not, by way of trade or otherwise, be lent, resold, hired out without the publisher's prior consent in any form of binding or cover other than that in which it is published and without a similar condition including this condition being imposed on the subsequent purchaser.

Preamble:
This is a hodgepodge of facts, opinions and musings that wandered through my consciousness during the past year or so. I found them interesting and so I share them with my friends in the hope that you may find some of interest – indeed, perhaps of surprise! And wonder: *"Is it possible?"* while remembering the words of Gabriel:
"*with God nothing will be impossible.*"

Side note:
An appendix contains some facts about the size of the Holy Land.

For me the Bible has always been somewhat of a mystery in more ways than one. It contains 73 books and comprises about 1,500 pages. The brief outline in the appendix may be of some help in reading it – or parts of it.

As usual, *E&OE!*
Winter 2024.

Inspiration?

What is this life if, full of reaction,
We have no time for mellow reflection.

No time to rest beneath the sky
And ask of ourselves, oh why, oh why?

No time to see the trees and grass.
And birds and rivers that blissfully pass.

No time to muse in the light of the moon,
For blessed slumber comes all too soon.

No time to behold the starry theatre
The pre-dawn art of the heavenly creator.

No time to think in the light of day,
For the world of care will have its way.

[Apologies to William Henry Davies.]

The basis for the teaching authority of the Catholic Church?

[*Or, what I cling to and trust.*]

One Holy, Catholic and Apostolic Church.

I am the good shepherd; I know my own and my own know me, as the Father knows me and I know the Father; and I lay down my life for the sheep. And I have other sheep, that are not of this fold; I must bring them also, and they will heed my voice. So, there shall be

<u>one</u> flock, <u>one</u> shepherd.

John 10:14-16.

Institution of the Papacy.

Simon Peter replied, "You are the Christ, the Son of the living God." And Jesus answered him, "Blessed are you, Simon Bar-Jona! For flesh and blood has not revealed this to you, but my Father who is in heaven. And I tell you,

you are Peter and on this rock I will build my church,

and the powers of death shall not prevail against it. I will give you the keys of the kingdom of heaven, and

whatever you bind on earth shall be bound in heaven,

and whatever you loose on earth shall be loosed in heaven."

Matthew 16:16-19.

Jesus said to Simon Peter, "Simon, son of John, do you love me more than these?" He said to him, "Yes, Lord; you know that I love you." He said to him,
"Feed my lambs."
A second time he said to him, "Simon, son of John, do you love me?" He said to him, "Yes, Lord; you know that I love you." He said to him,
"Tend my sheep."
He said to him the third time, "Simon, son of John, do you love me?" Peter was grieved because he said to him the third time, "Do you love me?" And he said to him, "Lord, you know everything; you know that I love you." Jesus said to him,
"Feed my sheep".
John 21:15-17.

Guidance in Truth by Holy Spirit.

*These things I have spoken to you, while I am still with you. But the Counsellor, the **Holy Spirit**, whom the Father will send in my name, he will teach you all things, and bring to your remembrance all that I have said to you.*
John 14:25-26.

*But when the Counsellor comes, whom I shall send to you from the Father, even the **Spirit of truth**, who proceeds from the Father, he will bear witness to* *me; and you also are witnesses, because you have been with me from the beginning.*

John 15:26-27.

Nevertheless I tell you the truth: it is to your advantage that I go away, for if I do not go away, the Counsellor will not come to you; but if I go, I will send him to you. And when he comes, he will convince the world concerning sin and righteousness and judgment: concerning sin, because they do not believe in me; concerning righteousness, because I go to the Father, and you will see me no more;
concerning judgment, because the ruler of this world is judged.
I have yet many things to say to you, but you cannot bear them now.
When the Spirit of truth comes, he will guide you into all the truth;
for he will not speak on his own authority, but whatever he hears he will speak, and he will declare to you the things that are to come. He will glorify me, for he will take what is mine and declare it to you. All that the Father has is mine; therefore I said that he will take what is mine and declare it to you.

John 16:7-15.

So, when they had come together, they asked him, "Lord, will you at this time restore the kingdom to Israel?" He said to them, "It is not for you to know

times or seasons which the Father has fixed by his own authority. But **you shall receive power when the Holy Spirit has come upon you**; *and you shall be my witnesses in Jerusalem and in all Judea and Samaria and to the end of the earth." And when he had said this, as they were looking on, he was lifted up, and a cloud took him out of their sight.*
Acts 1:6-9.

When the day of Pentecost had come, they were all together in one place. And suddenly a sound came from heaven like the rush of a mighty wind, and it filled all the house where they were sitting. And there appeared to them tongues as of fire, distributed and resting on each one of them. And **they were all filled with the Holy Spirit** *and began to speak in other tongues, as the Spirit gave them utterance.*
Acts 2:1-4.

Mission.

All authority in heaven and on earth has been given to me. Go therefore and make disciples of all nations, baptizing them in the name of the Father and of the Son and of the Holy Spirit, teaching them to observe all that I have commanded you; and lo, I am with you always, to the close of the age.
Matthew 28:18-20.

Why should we believe?

For an exposition of why the Gospels are true history and a true (though somewhat brief and selective) biography refer to *The Case for Jesus: The Biblical and Historical Evidence for Christ* by Dr. Brant Pitre.

But this knowledge is not sufficient to cause/allow one to believe.

A person needs Faith. And, Faith is a gift! As Jesus said to Peter:

Blessed are you, Simon Bar-Jona! For flesh and blood has not revealed this to you, but my Father who is in heaven.

But, don't worry - at Baptism we receive the gifts of faith, hope and charity. At Confirmation these graces are strengthened by the further gifts of wisdom, understanding, right judgment, courage, knowledge, reverence and wonder and awe of our Lord.

Note: Be assured that the author of this compilation does not speak with authority. Readers are exhorted to refer to the Catechism of the Catholic Church (*CCC*). Intense and extensive work went into its preparation over many years and it was approved for publication by Pope St. John XXIII on 25 June 1992.
It is a monumental and inexhaustible *magnum opus*.

The Eucharist
"is the source and summit of the Christian life".

> *"I am the Alpha and the Omega,
> the first and the last,
> the beginning and the end."*
>
> Revelation 22:13.

The other sacraments, and indeed all ecclesiastical ministries and works of the apostolate, are bound up with the Eucharist and are oriented towards it. For in the blessed Eucharist is contained the whole spiritual good of the Church, namely Christ himself, our Pasch.

The Eucharist passovers the efficacious sign and sublime cause of that communication in the divine life and that unity of the People of God by which the Church is kept in being. It is the culmination both of God's action sanctifying the world in Christ and of the worship men offer to Christ and through him to the Father in the Holy Spirit.

Finally, by the Eucharistic celebration we already unite ourselves with the heavenly liturgy and anticipate eternal life, when God will be all in all.

In brief, the Eucharist is the sum and summary of our faith: *"Our way of thinking is attuned to the Eucharist, and the Eucharist in turn confirms our way of thinking"*.

LITURGY

A public service, duty, or work. In Scripture it refers to the religious duties to be performed by priests and Levites in the Temple, especially those related to the Sacrifice; in Christian use among the Eastern Churches it means the Eucharistic Sacrifice.

In present day usage liturgy is the official public worship of the Church and is thus distinguished from private devotion. It is the special title of the Eucharist, and the administration of the sacraments with the annexed use of the sacramentals.

Emmaus.
When he was at table with them, he took the bread and blessed, and broke it, and gave it to them.
*And **their eyes were opened** and they recognized him;*
And they rose that same hour and returned to Jerusalem; and they found the eleven gathered together and those who were with them...
*Then they told what had happened on the road, and how **he was known to them in the breaking of the bread**.*

Luke 24.

Sacrifice in the Old and New Testaments.

> *Sacrifice is a ritualised offering of self.*

Typology in the Old Testament.

The Church, as early as apostolic times, and then constantly in her Tradition, has illuminated the unity of the divine plan in the two Testaments through typology, which discerns in God's works of the Old Covenant prefiguration of what he accomplished in the fullness of time in the person of his incarnate Son. (Catechism of the Catholic Church – 128).

The Bread of the Presence (Face).
(An Old Testament herald of the everlasting covenant.)

Then Moses and Aaron, Nadab, and Abihu, and seventy of the elders of Israel went up, and they saw the God of Israel… **they beheld God, and ate and drank**…

The Lord said to Moses, *"Speak to the people of Israel… And let them make me a sanctuary, that I may dwell in their midst…"*

*"Moreover, you shall make the **tabernacle**…"*

"And you shall make a table of acacia wood; two cubits shall be its length, a cubit its breadth, and a cubit and a half its height… You shall overlay it with pure gold…"

*"And you shall take fine flour, and bake **twelve cakes** of it; two tenths of an ephah shall be in each cake. And you shall set them in two rows, six in a row, upon the table of pure gold. And you shall put pure frankincense with each row, that*

*it may go with **the bread as a memorial portion to be offered by fire to the Lord.***
Every sabbath day *Aaron shall set it in order before the Lord continually on behalf of the people of Israel as a covenant for ever.*
*And it shall be for Aaron and his sons, and **they shall eat it in a holy place*** *[along with drinking wine], since it is for him a most holy portion out of the offerings by fire* [incense] *to the Lord, a perpetual due…"*
*"And you shall set the bread of the Presence on the table before me **always**…"*

"Three times a year shall all your males see the face of the Lord, the LORD God of Israel"

Feasts of Passover, Pentecost, and Tabernacles.
They [the priests] used to lift it [the Golden Table] up and exhibit the Bread of the Presence on it to those who came up for the festivals, saying to them,
"Behold, God's love for you!"
(Babylonian Talmud, Menahoth).

Then:
For more than a thousand years the priests of Jews offered bread and wine to God every week. Then they ate the bread and drank the wine.

Now:
In the Mass all Catholics can participate in the redemptive offering of his life by Jesus on Calvary where he appears to us under the forms foreshadowed in the Old Testament.

Eucharist.

The Council of Trent (1545 to 1563).

The Council teaches and openly and plainly professes that after the consecration of bread and wine, our Lord Jesus Christ, true God and true man, is truly, really and substantially contained in the august sacrament of the Holy Eucharist under the appearance of those sensible things.

The sacrifice of Christ and the sacrifice of the Eucharist are *one single sacrifice.*
The victim is one and the same; the same now offers through the ministry of priests, who then offered himself on the cross; only the **manner** of offering is different.

CCC 1367.

And since in this divine sacrifice which is celebrated in the Mass, the same Christ who offered himself in a bloody manner on the altar of the cross is contained and is offered in an unbloody manner…this sacrifice is truly propitiatory.

Council of Trent.

For our imagination.
"Heaven on Earth"

In the Mass the church building becomes an earthly representation of heaven and as St. John Chrysostom says:

The angels surround the priest. The whole sanctuary and the space before the altar are filled with the heavenly Powers come to honour Him who is present upon the altar.

Think now of what kind of choir you are going to enter. Although vested with a body, you have been judged worthy to join the Powers of heaven in singing the praises of Him who is Lord of all.

Behold the royal table. The angels serve at it. The Lord Himself is present.

And that is why at the Preface we sing:

And so, **with Angels and Archangels, with Thrones and Dominions, and with all the hosts and Powers of heaven,** *we sing the hymn of your glory, as without end we acclaim: Holy, Holy, Holy Lord God of Hosts …*

Note for my grandchildren.

Your guardian angel is ecstatically joyous every time you bring her/him to Mass. If you listen carefully you will hear *"Go raibh míle maith agat, mo chara daor."*

The Bread of Life.
[*Eucharist*]
[Brief extract from John 6]

"For the **bread of God** is that which comes down from heaven and **gives life** to the world."

"I am the bread of life.

Whosoever comes to me will never be hungry, and whoever believes in me will never be thirsty.

I have come down from heaven

not to do my own will but the will of him who sent me.

Very truly, I tell you, whoever believes has eternal life.

I am the bread of life.

Your ancestors ate the manna[1] in the wilderness, and they died. This is the bread that comes down from heaven, so that one may eat of it and not die.

I am the living bread that came down from heaven.
Whoever eats of this bread will live forever, and

the bread that I will give for the life of the world is my flesh."

"Very truly, I tell you, unless you eat the flesh of the Son of Man and drink his blood, you have no life in you.

Those who eat my flesh and drink my blood have eternal life,

---
[1] "*Manna*" means "*What is it?*"

and I will raise them up on the last day, for my flesh is true food, and my blood is true drink."

He said these things while he was teaching in a synagogue at Capernaum.

When many of his disciples heard it, they said,

"This teaching is difficult; who can accept it?"

But Jesus, being aware that his disciples were complaining about it, said to them,

"Does this offend you? Then what if you were to see the Son of Man ascending to where he was before?

It is the spirit that gives life; the flesh is useless.

The words that I have spoken to you are spirit and life. But among you there are some who do not believe."

For Jesus knew from the beginning who were the ones who did not believe and who was the one who would betray him. And he said, "For this reason I have told you that no one can come to me unless it is granted by the Father."

Because of this many of his disciples turned back and no longer went about with him.

So, Jesus asked the twelve,

"Do you also wish to go away?"

Simon Peter answered him,

"Lord, to whom can we go?

You have the words of eternal life. We have come to believe and know that you are the Holy One of God.

> Peter's is our great prayer when we are beset by doubts
>
> ***Lord, to whom can I go?***

Fulfilment of promise of *Bread of Life.*

St. Paul's 1 Corinthians	Mark	Matthew	Luke
For I received from the Lord what I also delivered to you, that the Lord Jesus on the night when he was betrayed took bread, and when he had given thanks, he broke it, and said, "This is my body which is for you. Do this in remembrance	And as they were eating, he took bread, and blessed, and broke it, and gave it to them, and said, *"Take; this is my body."* And he took a cup, and when he had given thanks he gave it to them, and they all drank of it. And he	Now as they were eating, Jesus took bread, and blessed, and broke it, and gave it to the disciples and said, *"Take, eat; this is my body."* And he took a cup, and when he had given thanks he gave it to them, saying, *"Drink of it, all of you; for*	And when the hour came, he sat at table, and the apostles with him. And he said to them, *"I have earnestly desired to eat this Passover with you before I suffer; for I tell you I shall not eat it until it is fulfilled in the kingdom of God."*

of me." In the same way also the cup, after supper, saying, *"This cup is the new covenant in my blood. Do this, as often as you drink it, in remembrance of me."*	said to them, *"This is my blood of the covenant, which is poured out for many".*	*this is my blood of the covenant, which is poured out for many for the forgiveness of sins."*	And he took a cup, and when he had given thanks he said, *"Take this, and divide it among yourselves; for I tell you that from now on I shall not drink of the fruit of the vine until the kingdom of God comes."* And he took bread, and when he had given thanks he broke it and gave it to them, saying, *"This is my body which is given for you. Do this in remembrance of me."* And likewise the cup after supper,

				saying, *"This cup which is poured out for you is the new covenant in my blood."*

Sacrifice in the New Testament.
Eucharist.
[Greek for *"Thanksgiving"*.]

Acts

And they devoted themselves to the apostles' teaching and fellowship, to the breaking of bread and the prayers.

And day by day, attending the temple together and breaking bread in their homes, they partook of food with glad and generous hearts,

On the first day of the week, when we met to break bread…

We humans make an offering to God.
[God returns infinitely more]

"Blessed are you, Lord God of all creation,
for through your goodness we have received
the bread we offer you:
fruit of the earth and work of human hands,
it will become for us the bread of life."

Bread comprises:	From God: the *"stuff"* of the bread = **substance**
	From us: thresh, knead and bake = **shape**
Be pleased, O God…to	We have made the shape

bless...this offering...so that it may become for us the Body and Blood of...Jesus Christ.	with matter given to us by the Creator. We pray to the Creator to change the substance of the bread.
*Make holy, therefore, these gifts, we pray, by sending down your Spirit upon them like the **dewfall**, so that they may become for us the Body and Blood of our Lord, Jesus Christ.*	An allusion to manna in Exodus 16:14: *in the morning there was a layer of **dew** around the camp. When the dew was gone, thin flakes like frost on the ground appeared.*
On the day He was to suffer, He took bread...in his hands and...giving You thanks, He said the blessing, broke the bread, and gave it to his disciples, saying,	Through the priest we recall an event that occurred at the Last Supper during the Passover.

Take this, all of you, and eat of it,
for this is My body,
which will be given up for you.
 	
[Mark 14:22-24.
Matthew 26:26-29.
Luke 22:19-21.
1 Corinthians 11:23-26.]
	Note: "*this*" and not "*this bread*"!
	The words spoken by Jesus in anticipation of the sacrifice of his life and fulfilling his promise to become for us the
	    Bread of Life come down
	    from Heaven.
	[John 6:35-69]

The Host now comprises:	From us:
	    Shape.
	From God:
	    glorified Jesus.

In return for our gift to God of bread (the substance of which he made)	God accepts the substance of the bread, replaces that substance with His glorified Son and will return it to us.
[What remains of our offering are the shape and accidents of bread.]	
"Do **This** In memory of me."	
And so, we do "***This***" every time we celebrate Mass.	
The consecrated bread is eaten by the celebrant and the congregation. This is truly mind boggling.	
"with God nothing will be impossible."	
The celebrant blesses the congregation and announces that the Mass is finished. *Ite missa est.* *Deo Gratias.*	

Holy Communion the source of real **LIFE**.

As I ponder the Holy Communion wafer in the palm of my hand I wonder at:
- This is God who created me;
- This is God who created the universe of billions of galaxies;
- This is the **living** body of a human who lived on Earth 2,000 years ago;
- This is the **living** body of a man who died out of love for me;
- This is the **living** body of a man who of his own power raised himself from the dead;
- This is the **living** body of a person who resides in heaven.
- This is the God-man who was tortured and killed to show me how much he loved me. Me!
- This is real **life.**

> *Jesus said,*
> *"All things are possible to him who believes."*
> We say: *"We believe; help our unbelief."*
> Gabriel said,
> *"For with God nothing will be impossible"*
> With Mary we should say,
> *"let it be to us according to your word."*

And my mind strays to a few awesome verses in chapter 6 of John's gospel:
> *He who eats my flesh and drinks my blood abides in me, and I in him.*

and

> *It is the spirit that gives **life**, the flesh is of no avail; the words that I have spoken to you are spirit and **life**.*

And thence to chapter 1:
> *In the beginning was the Word, and the Word was with God, and the Word was God.*
> *In him was **life**, and the **life** was the light of men.*

And there it is:

Lifeness

Hadn't Jesus said:
- *the **bread of God** is that which comes down from heaven, and gives **life** to the world*
- *I am the bread of **life***
- *I am the bread of **life**.*
- *I am the **living bread** which came down from heaven*
- *Truly, truly, I say to you, unless you eat the flesh of the Son of man and drink his blood, you have no **life** in you*
- *he who eats my flesh and drinks my blood has **eternal life***
- *He who eats my flesh and drinks my blood abides in me, and I in him.*
- *he who eats me will **live** because of me*
- *he who eats this bread will **live** for ever.*

Jesus makes an appeal to the most basic human instinct:

Self-survival

We eat physical food and drink physical liquid to survive physically.

Jesus tells us that we need spiritual food and spiritual drink to survive (have life in us) spiritually – forever.

And, before he dies, rises, and ascends into heaven he gives us access to this food, that is, to himself, under the appearance of bread to be with us until the end of time.

And that is why, in the prayer that he gave us, he asks us to pray:

Give us this day our ~~daily~~ epiousios (super-substantial) food.

And why he assures us:

And remember, I am with you always, to the end of the age.

Prayer of St. Thomas Aquinas
Before receiving Holy Communion.

Almighty and ever-living God, I approach the sacrament of your only begotten Son, our Lord Jesus Christ.

I come sick to the doctor of life, unclean to the fountain of mercy, blind to the radiance of eternal light, and poor and needy to the Lord of heaven and earth.

Lord, in your great generosity, heal my sickness, wash away my defilement, enlighten my blindness, enrich my poverty, and clothe my nakedness.

May I receive the Bread of angels, the King of kings and Lord of lords, with humble reverence, with the purity and faith, the repentance and love, and the determined purpose that will help to bring me to salvation.

May I receive the Sacrament of the Lord's Body and Blood, and its reality and power.

Kind God, may I receive the body of your only begotten Son, our Lord Jesus Christ, born from the womb of the Virgin Mary, and so be received into his mystical body and numbered among his members.

Loving Father, as on my earthly pilgrimage I now receive your beloved Son under the veil of a sacrament, may I one day see Him face to face in glory, who lives and reigns with you for ever.

Amen.

Prayer of St. Thomas Aquinas
After receiving Holy Communion.

I thank You, Lord, Almighty Father, Everlasting God, for having been pleased, through no merit of mine, but of Your great mercy alone, to feed me, a sinner, and Your unworthy servant, with the precious Body and Blood of Your Son, our Lord Jesus Christ.

I pray that this Holy Communion may not be for my judgment and condemnation, but for my pardon and salvation.

Let this Holy Communion be to me an armour of faith and a shield of good will, a cleansing of all vices, and a rooting out of all evil desires.

May it increase love and patience, humility and obedience, and all virtues.

May it be a firm defence against the evil designs of all my visible and invisible enemies, a perfect quieting of all the desires of soul and body.

May this Holy Communion bring about a perfect union with You, the one true God, and at last enable me to reach eternal bliss when You will call me.

I pray that You bring me, a sinner, to the indescribable Feast where You, with Your Son and the Holy Spirit, are to Your Saints true light, full blessedness, everlasting joy, and perfect happiness.

Through the same Christ our Lord.
Amen.

Our Gospels.

Since the 1780s the first three books of the New Testament have been called the **Synoptic Gospels** because they are so similar in structure, content, and wording that they can easily be set side by side to provide a synoptic comparison of their content.

Literally the titles *"Christ"* (Greek word) and *"Messiah"* (Hebrew word) each means *"the anointed one"* and refers to the ancient practice of anointing kings with oil when they took the throne.

Recently I came across two matters which changed and enhanced my readings of the Gospels. One was the relationship between John's Gospel and the synoptic Gospels. The other was one which had a significant effect on how Jesus announced his messiahship and the coming of the Kingdom of God.

Also recommended is the approach advised by Yeshua:

Truly, I say to you, whoever does not receive the kingdom of God like a child shall not enter it.

Mark 10:15

This does not mean that one should be *"childish"*!

St. Augustine suggests that one of three reasons apply if on reading a Biblical text you think it is wrong:
- ➢ An error was made in translation; or
- ➢ An error was made in copying; or
- ➢ You do not understand the text rightly!!!

Why does John's Gospel seem somewhat different from those of Matthew, Mark and Luke?

The last Evangelist wishes for his part to supplement what the first three have either omitted or barely touched on. This explains his silence about the parables and many of the miracles which are recorded by the synoptists, and about the institution of the Last Supper. This accounts, too, for his giving us words and deeds of Jesus which had been left out of the other Gospels, especially those of the eucharistic and high-priestly discourses, and those concerning the washing of the disciples' feet, additional features of the scene of the Last Supper, as given in the synoptics. Also, the detailed accounts of the activity of Jesus in Judea and Jerusalem, which are rendered in a more condensed form by the synoptists, as well as the concise summary of his Galilean achievements, which had been already minutely described in the first Gospels, are all comprehensible from this point of view.

Another aim is also discoverable in John's Gospel. The synoptists wrote before the destruction of the Jewish nation. They still hoped always to win over the chosen people to the kingdom of God. They therefore laid as much stress as possible on the points of connection between the Old and New Testaments—the purely human element in Christ which united Jew and Christian.

John takes his pen in hand, after God's judgement has already fallen upon Jerusalem, and after the Church has, fortunately, wholly freed itself from the embrace of the dead synagogue. Accordingly, he accentuates the points of separation between them—the thoroughly non-Jewish element in Christianity, whereby the Church revealed itself in its full spiritual independence and thus became sympathetic to the pagans. Even in his wording and representation of Christian doctrine, John, who is writing in Asia Minor, comes as closely as possible to classic ways of thinking, feeling and speaking, and even adopts the Greek idea and expressions about the Logos, because these seemed to him admirably adapted to serve as a vessel for the doctrine of the incarnate Son of God. The incarnate Son of God was, on the whole, the great thesis of this prophet among the Evangelists. While the synoptists, out of consideration for the Jews, had to emphasize the human side, and the Old Testament's Messianic conception of the Saviour, John, in opposition to the Jewish-Christian heresy, which represented Christ as merely a man, was obliged to defend the supernatural grandeur and essential divinity of Jesus. And not only that; in mind and heart alike he feels the necessity of revealing to men, in his entire glory and sublimity, the Master, whom he loved supremely, and whom he, better than anyone else, had learned to know from a most intimate companionship.

That was indeed one more reason why John preferred for his portrayal the later Judaic and Jerusalem period, during which the divine-human manifestations had already made further progress than in the Galilean period, when the Lord first imparted to his disciples the fundamental ideas of the new plan of salvation. The Apostle also, in accordance with his purpose, selects for narration those episodes which contain the most striking proofs of his thesis. Even the miracles are chosen from the *"point of view of the self-revelation and manifestation of the glory of the Son of God."*

The Christ of John is the true Son of God, who, out of love for us, has come down to earth from the glory of the Father, and has become flesh in order, as a human, to live with humans and for humans.

The Christ of the synoptists is the true Son of Man, flesh of our flesh and blood of our blood, but sustained by his Messianic dignity, and thoroughly imbued with divine power and essence, in order to lift us up to God.

Thus are the alleged contradictions between John and the synoptists are solved by the higher unity of the entire Gospel. From this it is evident that there is no justification for the idea that Christ and Christology are in John's Gospel essentially different in character from those in the synoptic Gospels.[2]

The so-called "*Messianic secret*" in Mark's gospel.

In the popular imagination of that time the Messiah was, first of all, a political liberator. As the Son of David, he was, by his mere appearance, to shatter with one blow the Roman yoke, re-establish the Jewish throne, and, as King of Israel, lead the people of the Law, and the life according to the Law, to triumph. Where such a frame of mind was prevalent it needed only a breath to cause the flame of national aspiration to flare up at once. A popular rumour of the presence of the Messiah—that is, of the national hero—would be sufficient to kindle boundless political enthusiasm and call forth a general "*Messianic*" revolution.

Willingly or unwillingly, Jesus would have been forced into the leadership of this if he had simply called himself the Messiah. A fatal conflict with the authorities would have put a **precipitous ending** to his scarcely begun career and frustrated his whole work.

In order to escape this premature catastrophe, he prevented the too precipitate proclamation of his Messiahship, and himself avoided assuming the name Messiah.

---

[2] Christ and the critics by Hilarin Felder.

It is true the first disciples, overpowered by the impression produced by his language and his personality, suspect in him at once the Messiah, and give him the Messianic title. *"We have found the Messiah!"* cries out Andrew to his brother Simon, after his first meeting with Jesus (John 1:41). *"We have found him of whom Moses in the Law and the Prophets did write,"* announces Philip to Nathanael (John 1:45). And shortly after his meeting with Jesus, Nathanael also confesses: *"Rabbi, thou art the Son of God; thou art the King of Israel"* (John 1:49).

The demons also seek to proclaim his Messiahship through the mouths of those they possessed. For *"they knew him"* (Mark 1:34), *"they knew that he was the Messiah"* (Luke 4:41), the *"Holy One of God,"* *"the Anointed One of God,"* the *"Son of God,"* the *"Son of the most high God,"* who had come to destroy them.?

Jesus accepts with joy the acknowledgement of the first disciples, although, as it proved later, it was only a joyful expression of faith and hope that the Master would prove himself to be the Messiah (John 1:50). Yet he substitutes for the titles *"Messiah"*, *"Prophet"*, *"King of Israel"* (to the Jews all these had the same significance) the title **"Son of Man."** Also, he does not contradict the utterances of the devils, although he admonishes them severely not to proclaim him publicly as the Messiah.[3]

---

[3] Christ and the critics by Hilarin Felder.

The Pharisaical and Rabbinical Concept of the Messiah.

In his book, *Christ and the critics*, Hilarin Felder gives us a comprehensive outline of the kind of Messiah (or *"Deliverer"*) expected by the Jews. They wanted a great warrior who, through overwhelming and ruthless warfare would make their nation the greatest in the world and King of all other nations. The following is a condensed version of Felder's outline.

The Pharisaical and rabbinical theology developed after the return from exile, reached its climax about the time of Jesus, and was thereupon edited in the writings of the Synagogue, and especially in the literature of the Talmud.

Note.
The Talmud is not in the Bible. It is a compilation of ancient teachings contained in 63 tractates (books) regarded as sacred and normative by Jews.
The Torah contains the first five books of the Bible – also called the Pentateuch.

At the first glance it seems strange that the rabbinical theology, and, with it, later Judaism, was not able to maintain itself at the height of that notion of the Messiah, entertained by the prophets. **It laid little stress any longer on the prophetic writings.**
In order to strengthen practical Jewish life as opposed to the influences of their pagan environment, the Law—that is, the 613 Torah commandments (for such was the number that the Scribes found in the Pentateuch)—became more and more exaggerated at the expense of the real meaning of the prophetical Messianic revelation.
According to the Rabbis the books of the Law contain the whole of religion, and the Torah is the revelation, in which

God has included everything that he in any way can reveal through all eternity. The Law existed even before the world, and, accordingly, God already circumcised Adam before he breathed into him the breath of life, while the prophetical and doctrinal books of Holy Scripture came only later and, as it were by chance. The books of the Law will also exist eternally, while all the rest of the revelation will at some future time pass out of validity and use.

This frightful exaggeration of the Law destroyed the whole prophetical expectation of salvation.

If the Mosaic Law—that is, the Law as interpreted by rabbinical and kabbalistic exegesis, as the highest good and the only thing which remains eternally—is all, then Mosaism can no longer be a means to the end of Messianic redemption, and no more a transient institution; it is then itself redemption and perfection.

According to this, Judaism was redeemed on Mount Sinai. This act of redemption was to be the end of God's dealings, and the nuptial relation which had been created thus between God and his people was to last for ever.

The aim of the historical development of the plan of salvation is, therefore, to get back again, through the fulfilment of the Law, what, through the episode of the golden calf, had been lost. It is no more a matter of inward justification and of an atoning redemption from sin;

sin, atonement, healing and justification, in the sense of Holy Scripture, are unknown to rabbinical theology.

The great means of redemption and the great act of redemption is excellence in matters of the Law, and that only. To complete this act of redemption is, however, not, of course, the work of the Messiah. The nation or individual must alone and on its own account make itself just through a mathematically strict balancing between debit and credit, between the demands of the Law and their fulfilment. These demands and fulfilments are noted down day by day, reckoned up, credited and balanced.

Only when the balance of all the individuals and of the whole nation corresponds to the budget of the Law—in other words, only when all Israel is justified and made holy—does the Messiah begin his work.

Then, and only then, will the Messiah appear, as the well-earned reward for fidelity to the Law; not as a grace, much less as an act of redemption.

His redeeming work—if one can still speak of it as such—consists in the fact that he, by word and example, encourages and perpetuates faithfulness to the Law. As a perfectly competent scribe, he will instruct all the people in the Torah, and even take upon himself its unbearable yoke; and he will be *"loaded down, like a mill, with fulfilments of rabbinical commandments."*

That is all. A great Rabbi—nothing more; that is the Messiah of the theology of the Synagogue.

But a Messiah who makes his appearance as a preacher of morals, and who accuses this people, so faithful to the Law, and, above all, the flower and intelligence of the nation—the Scribes and Pharisees—of guilt and sin, is at once condemned as a false Messiah.

Should he once disclose the necessity of a religious regeneration for Israel, or should he wish to proclaim a religion surpassing the Mosaism of the Rabbis, he is a traitor to the Holy of Holies, a blasphemer. But also, even the censure, and still more the violation of one single rabbinical iota, the healing of a sick man, or the plucking an ear of corn upon the Sabbath, association with a publican, or the omission of an ablution, marked him as a disciple of Beelzebub.

In the opinion of the Rabbis, the kingdom of Heaven itself

came down to earth with the Lord on Sinai. Since God had taken up his abode in the midst of his people. His dominion assured not only Israel's predominance over the Gentiles, who served him as his footstool, but it created paradisaical conditions of every kind. God's nearness banished all the consequences of original sin and re-established the blessed primitive state of the Garden of Eden in this terrestrial kingdom of Heaven, until the earth should be merged into heaven itself, and time into eternity. Thus, did Nomism imagine the first redemptive kingdom on Sinai to have been, and thus, it logically imagined would be also its rehabilitation by the Messiah.

The Messiah will appear, drive back the enemies of Israel, compel the Gentiles to respect the Torah, and establish the Messianic dominion.

Jerusalem, the capital of the kingdom, will, at the same time, be the metropolis of all the cities of the world.

The vast Roman Empire, which arose only on account of Israel's sins, will lie in ruins at his feet.

The non-Roman pagan nations will be obliged to pay tribute to him and to the pious Israelites, as vassal states.

To serve the Messiah and the Jews in Palestine will be the sole *raison d'étre* of the nations living outside Palestine.

As a beneficent Messianic king, the Messiah offers himself only to the children of Abraham and only in the Promised Land.

All the sensuous delights of the Israelitish kingdom of the Torah ever dreamed of will be realized—the removal by the Messiah of every kind of sickness and distress, wonderful physical beauty and vitality for the children of Israel, and a fabulous productivity of soil and plants etc., etc. Shall it therefore be said that the rabbinical attitude towards

Rabbinical Judaism has never failed to recognize the importance of its historical plan of salvation. It was, as we have said, convinced that the Messiah would lead the Jews to the exact observation of the religious Law of God in the Torah, and also would bring those who were not Israelites to recognize it.

The supremacy of the Torah, which, according to rabbinical interpretation, was one with the supremacy of God, was to make itself felt everywhere over the whole earth. So far as this the Pharisaical idea of the Messiah was thoroughly religious, and even religious in a universal sense.

And not only in theory, but also in the practical conduct of life, did the Jews show a great, in fact, an unheard-of zeal for the hoped-for *"kingdom of God."* One must allow that under the leadership of the Pharisees they were more enthusiastic for the kingdom of God than ever, and sought to usher it in, not merely through a punctual observation of the Law, but through an acceptance of the rabbinical *"yoke."*

The immense mistake lay in the fact that this Messianic conception, whether practical or theoretical, was applied to a kingdom of God which in a secular and political sense had acquired a changed value. The Judaists understood by this, in spite of all pious phrases and Pharisaical hypocrisy, essentially a sudden change of things in the sense of the materialized, thoroughly worldly and particularly Jewish-Davidic supremacy. **They endured the Law and *"yoke"* principally because these were the means to this political and national purpose**.

And even Jehovah, who was to assume the government of Israel, must for this purpose, place himself exclusively at the service of the Jewish national aspirations. He must put himself entirely under the orders of the Jewish Sanhedrim.

By the time of Christ, the Jewish kingdom of God and expectations concerning the Messiah had sunk to a political and material level.

The main thing, the essential element in the Messiah is his Davidic kingdom, the secular power with which he is to rule Israel, shatter its enemies and purify Jerusalem from the Gentiles.

We need only to open the Gospel to become convinced that this conception of the kingdom and activity of the Messiah was by no means an isolated instance. Wherever the Scribes and Pharisees appear in the Gospels, and wherever Jesus comes at all into contact with official Judaism in province or capital, we recognize the same materialized notion of the Messiah.

The rabbinical-Jewish Messiah is also, on that very account, merely a man, both in origin and by nature. Only the name of the Messiah—that is, the plan of his mission—is ancient. It is true, together with this ideal, the Palestine theology admits also a real pre-existence of the soul of the Messiah. This was, however, only in consequence of the rabbinical anthropology, which believes all human souls to have been created before the world, and kept in a sort of store-house in the seventh heaven until the moment of their union with the body.

The Messiah is therefore a pre-existent and transcendental being in no other sense than all other men are. Also, the doctrine of the purely human origin and nature of the Messiah was not at all a more or less disseminated dogma, but was the common view of the rabbinical-Jewish theology. The Jew Trypho assures St Justin very positively: *"We all expect the Messiah as a man born from human parents, and as one who will receive from Elias, as soon as the latter shall appear, the kingly consecration."*

If now we compare these rabbinical views, which were current among the contemporaries of Jesus, with those of the Old Testament, the result is a very wide difference. The narrow, national, materialistic power of the Pharisaical Messianic kingdom, pertaining to this world only, stands in striking contrast to the world-embracing spiritual kingdom of God. It is true that it based itself upon the religious fundamental Law of the Torah and had a theocratic character, but in principle it was conceived as thoroughly earthly and political.

The figure of the suffering and dying Servant of God was naturally no longer suited to this frame. It was the greatest conceivable annoyance to the Jews.

The supernatural and supernational Son of Man of Daniel became also detached from the Pharisaical notion of the Messiah, not to speak of Emmanuel.

Only the Son of David remained, the purely earthly and Jewishly interpreted offspring of the great king, who was to lead the national power of the Torah to victory.

Reading the Gospels.

The authors of the Gospels wrote for people of their time and so presumed that readers would be familiar with first century Jewish lifestyles, customs and mores and with the Law and the Prophets. If, in our day, some two thousand years later, we do not have knowledge of these then many implications and allusions in the Gospels are overlooked by us. We don't, as they say in Dublin, *"get it"*.

We cannot perceive the depth of meaning in these Gospels or the Epistles without a familiarity with Jewish lifestyle of that time and their understanding of the books of the Old Testament (*the Law and the Prophets*). A particular example is their understanding (or, more correctly misunderstanding) of what the Messiah would be – this was discussed above.

We also need to be aware of those who seek to mislead us by suggesting that some parts of the Gospels are later interpolations. Weren't we warned: *"Behold, I am sending you out as sheep in the midst of wolves, so be wise as serpents and innocent as doves"*.

An interpolation, in relation to ancient manuscripts, is an entry or passage in a text that was alleged to have not been written by the original author but inserted by a later scribe when making a copy of the book. For example, many speculators will conjecture that Matthew 16:16-29 (Peter the Rock on which the church is built) and/or Matthew 28:19-20 (Apostolic mission) are interpolations.

Such postulations are *"guesses"* since their veracity is not capable of proof other than scholarly opinion. They will be suggested with a beguilingly seductive argument. In many cases the position is that if the word or phrase had in fact been present in the original document then the scholar's hypothesis would fail!

I have to confess to harbouring an unkind thought as to the possibility of selfish reasons for such opinions. If one believes that the Catholic Church is correct in its manifesto then one brings on oneself a heap of requirements that can be at loggerheads with physical appetites. If, on the other hand, one considers that atheism or agnosticism is appropriate then one appears to have more freedom. After all, is it not true that *I am the centre of the universe*? Another unkind thought is that one can make quite a lot of money publishing books containing sensational new claims – witness *Chariots of the Gods* or *The Da Vinci Code* as a somewhat extreme examples.

A personal opinion:

It seems to me that the gospels are sometimes somewhat terse in descriptions of events. I do not say this as a criticism. After all, St. Ignatius in his Exercises recommends praying with one's imagination (which he calls contemplation) as a very active way of praying that engages the mind and heart and stirs up thoughts and emotions.[4]

The manuscripts of the gospels lacked word spacing, so words, sentences, and paragraphs would be a continuous string of letters (scriptio continua). Indeed, there were even line breaks in the middle of words. There were no capital letters. Scholars have added chapter and verse headings, commas, full stops and paragraph breaks etc. because

otherwiseitwouldbedifficulttoreadintelligently

The gospels also seem to be somewhat short of explanations on occasion - I suppose that is because as John said at the end of his gospel:

---

[4] Lectio Divina.

But there are also many other things which Jesus did; were every one of them to be written, I suppose that the world itself could not contain the books that would be written.

For example, it is strange to me that Matthew, Mark and Luke do not make a reference to the washing of the apostles' feet before the Last Supper. John does, but, John does not make any reference to the words of consecration. While all of the writers of the synoptic gospels mention the words of consecration, they do not give any detail of Yeshua's other words which John reports at some length. This matter was discussed above.

So, for example, there follows the text (in italics) of the Last Supper (mostly Luke 22:1-23) with my interpolations.

The Last Supper.

You will recall that following the raising to life of Lazarus: *the Chief priests and the Pharisees gathered the council. Caiaphas, who was high priest that year, said to them*
    "It is expedient for you that one man should die for the people."
So from that day on they took counsel how to put him to death. Jesus therefore no longer went about openly among the Jews, but went from there (Jerusalem) *to the country near the wilderness, to a town called Ephraim; and there he stayed with the disciples.*
The chief priests and the Pharisees had given orders that if anyone knew where he was, he should let them know, so that they might arrest him.

Doesn't this seem to be a very strange thing for seventy-two priests to do? They were supposed to be holy men. They spent their days praying to God from sunup to sunset and offering sacrifices to God. Later, when the high priest questioned Jesus about his disciples and his teaching. Jesus answered him: *"I have spoken openly to the world; I have always taught in synagogues and in the temple, where all Jews come together; I have said nothing secretly. Why do you ask me? Ask those who have heard me, what I said to them; they know what I said."* (That did not go down well! And, it may be noted, none of Jesus' disciples were called as witnesses during his trial.) The priests had previously sent their most learned scholars to trip Jesus up in regard to his exegesis of teachings in the Law and the Prophets. To the delight and astonishment of the crowd he had confounded these experts, even going so far as to observe: *"you know neither the scriptures nor the power of God."*

> Previously he had berated the scribes and Pharisees (Lk. 11:25-54) and... *the scribes and the Pharisees began to press him hard, and to provoke him to speak of many things, lying in wait for him, to catch at something he might say.*
> As far as they were concerned Jesus could not be the Messiah – that is, as they understood what the Messiah would be.
> It is difficult to understand how they could take the fatal risk of denying his Divinity without, as Nicodemus had counselled, *"first giving him a hearing and learning what he does".*
> One can readily suspect that there was an interloper *returning at an opportune time* to manipulate the Sanhedrin, namely, Satan. He had failed during Jesus' forty days in the desert.

Six days before the Passover, Jesus came to Bethany (about 2 miles from Jerusalem).

> The feast of the *"Passover"* was celebrated every year on ONE day in April to remember the Exodus when Moses had led the Jews out of slavery in Egypt after the killing of all of the first born in that land with the exception of those first born on whose doorposts had been wiped the blood of a lamb, that is, the doorposts of the Jews.
> The feast of *"Unleavened bread"* was celebrated the following day and lasted for SEVEN days.

Now the feast of Unleavened Bread drew near, which is called the Passover. And the chief priests and the scribes were seeking how to put him to death; for they feared the people.

Then Satan entered into Judas called Iscariot, who was of the number of the twelve; he went away and conferred with the chief priests and officers how he might betray him to them. And they were glad, and engaged to give him money. So he agreed, and sought an opportunity to betray him to them in the absence of the multitude.

Then came the first day of the feast of Unleavened Bread, on which the Passover lamb had to be sacrificed in the Temple in Jerusalem. It was mandatory for Jews to celebrate this feast every year and to do so in Jerusalem.
It was also mandatory that the Passover meal be celebrated in the city of Jerusalem. Indeed Jesus had observed this ordinance every year since his childhood.

> Since the feast of Passover had to be celebrated in Jerusalem the population increased to a great amount. The historian Josephus suggests that it was 2.5 million. But most commentators reckon that this is somewhat exaggerated. In any event it would be teeming with visitors and animals and many would have been staying in tents on the hill up to Jerusalem. And it would be bustling with activity as people sought to purchase lambs for their families. Hence the arrangements made by Jesus. It was, as they say *all cloak and dagger*!

So Jesus sent Peter and John, saying, "Go and prepare the Passover (meal) *for us, that we may eat it."* (None of the disciples knew of the arrangements that Jesus had made for the supper or where it would be held). *They said to him, "Where will you have us prepare it?"*
He said to them, "Behold, when you have entered the city, (probably by the Golden Gate) *a man carrying a jar of water will meet you* (probably at the Golden Gate); *follow him into*

the house which he enters, and tell the householder, 'The Teacher says to you, Where is the guest room, where I am to eat the Passover with my disciples?'
And he will show you a large upper room furnished; there make ready." And they went, and found it as he had told them; and they prepared the Passover (meal). They were not to tell the other disciples about the arrangement. This was because Jesus knew that Judas meant to betray him to the Chief Priests and Jesus did not intend for this to happen before celebration of the Passover meal which was to be his Last Supper.

Now before the feast of the Passover (meal), *when Jesus knew that his hour had come to depart out of this world to the Father, having loved his own who were in the world, he loved them to the end. And during supper, when the devil had already put it into the heart of Judas Iscariot, Simon's son, to betray him, Jesus, knowing that the Father had given all things into his hands, and that he had come from God and was going to God, rose from supper, laid aside his garments, and girded himself with a towel. Then he poured water into a basin, and began to wash the disciples' feet, and to wipe them with the towel with which he was girded.* [The work of the lowliest of servants].

And then *he sat at table.*
And he said to them, "I have earnestly desired to eat this Passover with you before I suffer;

One has to interject here. God the Son (the Word who created the universe) earnestly ***desires*** to eat this meal with his disciples. "*Desires*"! It seems that this must be a very special meal. Something fundamental. And, of course it is!

for I tell you I shall not eat it until it is fulfilled in the kingdom of God."

> And he told them many things as recorded at some length in John chapters 13 to 17 about the coming of the Holy Spirit and that they would enjoy eternal life with him in heaven some of which are cited in the following passage.

When Judas had gone out, Jesus said, now is the Son of man glorified, and in him God is glorified...

A new commandment I give to you, that you love one another; even as I have loved you, that you also love one another...

Let not your hearts be troubled; believe in God, believe also in me.

In my Father's house are many rooms; if it were not so, would I have told you that I go to prepare a place for you? And when I go and prepare a place for you, I will come again and will take you to myself, that where I am you may be also...

If you love me, you will keep my commandments. And I will pray the Father, and he will give you another Counsellor... I will not leave you desolate; I will come to you...

If a man loves me, he will keep my word, and my Father will love him, and we will come to him and make our home with him. He who does not love me does not keep my words; and the word which you hear is not mine but the Father's who sent me...

The Counsellor, the Holy Spirit, whom the Father will send in my name will teach you all things, and bring to your remembrance all that I have said to you...

Peace I leave with you; my peace I give to you; not as the world gives do I give to you. Let not your hearts be troubled, neither let them be afraid...
I am the true vine, and my Father is the vinedresser.
As the Father has loved me, so have I loved you; abide in my love...
This is my commandment, that you love one another as I have loved you. Greater love has no man than this, that a man lay down his life for his friends...
This I command you, to love one another...
But when the Counsellor comes, whom I shall send to you from the Father, even the Spirit of truth, who proceeds from the Father, he will bear witness to me...
Nevertheless I tell you the truth: it is to your advantage that I go away, for if I do not go away, the Counsellor will not come to you; but if I go, I will send him to you...
When the Spirit of truth comes, he will guide you into all the truth; for he will not speak on his own authority, but whatever he hears he will speak, and he will declare to you the things that are to come...
A little while, and you will see me no more; again a little while, and you will see me...
Truly, truly, I say to you, if you ask anything of the Father, he will give it to you in my name...but be of good cheer, I have overcome the world....
Father, I desire that they also, whom thou hast given me, may be with me where I am, to behold my glory which thou hast given me in thy love for me before the foundation of the world.

I imagine that he then drew their minds back to the day on which he had miraculously multiplied the five loaves and two fish to feed over five thousand people and to the following night on which he had walked on water thus demonstrating his divine power over the wind and the sea.

And then, I imagine, to his discourse on the Bread of Life in the synagogue in Capernaum [John Chapter 6] and the necessity to eat his flesh and drink his blood. Many disciples had left him because they had been distraught at such a prospect. The reason that they could not accept this saying was because they did not believe that he, as the Bread of Life come down from heaven, was the Son of God for whom, as the angel Gabriel had said to Mary,
with God nothing will be impossible
Peter had already accepted this when, in response to Jesus' question: *But who do you say that I am?* said:

You are the Christ, the Son of the living God

And in Capernaum, in response to Jesus' question, *Do you also wish to go away?*
although he was also distraught, Peter said:

Lord, to whom shall we go?
You have the words of eternal life, and we have believed, and have come to know,
that you are the Holy One of God.

[Note: It seems likely that Judas Iscariot did not believe that Jesus was divine or that he was the promised Messiah. *Jesus answered them, "Did I not choose you, the twelve, and one of you is a devil?" He spoke of Judas the son of Simon Iscariot, for he, one of the twelve, was to betray him.*]

And now Jesus would show them how they could eat his flesh and drink his blood under the appearances of and sensing only bread and wine and, in Paul's words:

be neither Jew nor Greek, neither slave nor free, neither male nor female, for all are one in Christ Jesus.

And he took a cup, and when he had given thanks he said, "Take this, and divide it among yourselves; for I tell you that from now on I shall not drink of the fruit of the vine until the kingdom of God comes."

And he took bread, and when he had given thanks he broke it and gave it to them, saying,
"This is my body which is given for you.
Do this in remembrance of me."
And likewise the cup after supper, saying,
"Drink of it, all of you; for this is my blood of the covenant, which is poured out for many for the forgiveness of sins. This cup which is poured out for you is the new covenant in my blood."

This is my body which is given for you.
Do this in remembrance of me.
And likewise, the cup after supper, saying, "This cup which is poured out for you is
the new covenant *in my blood".*

What can have been going through the minds of the apostles? Here they are, sitting with Jesus, and he is telling them that what they are eating is him! A fragment broken off from a loaf of bread! How could this be? Isn't he there in front of me? How can he also be in eleven other places at the same time? And, even if this is possible, for what reason should I

eat him? And I am to drink his blood! What is going on? Don't we have the the Noahic, the Abrahamic, the Mosaic, and the Davidic Covenants? What does he mean by *"New Covenant?"*. But, as Peter said, "we *know that you are the Holy One of God."*
I trust you, Lord, for to whom else can I go?

And when they had sung a hymn, they went out across the Kidron Valley to the Mount of Olives. And they went to a garden which was called Gethsemane.

Now, that is just me and my ramblings. I hope it may be of some help – BUT it is best to read and contemplate the actual inspired accounts given to us by the evangelists. It is humbling how often another reading reveals a deeper meaning, a connection, even a *eureka* moment.

The Last Supper was a precursor to Jesus' passion, death and Resurrection. Let us back up a little to the beginning.

The Annunciation and aftermath.
[*With my interpolations.*]

> *In the days of Herod, king of Judea, there was a priest named Zechariah. Now while he was serving as priest before God* [in the holy place beside the Tabernacle] *there appeared to him an angel of the Lord who said to him,*
> *"Do not be afraid, Zechariah, for your prayer is heard, and your wife Elizabeth will **bear you a son**, and you shall **call his name John**."*
> *After these days his wife Elizabeth conceived, and for*

In the sixth month the angel Gabriel was sent from God to a town in Galilee named Nazareth,
to a virgin
betrothed to a man
whose name was Joseph, of the [Royal] *house of David: and the virgin's name was Mary.*
And he came to her and said,
"Hail, O favoured one, the Lord is with you!"
But she was greatly troubled at the saying, and considered in her mind what sort of greeting this might be.

> **Greatly** *troubled*?
> What form would the angel have taken? Where was teenage Mary? At home preparing a meal? In the garden? Presumably she was alone. I would be perturbed if this happened to me. Probably a bit terrified. What does "*favoured one*" mean?

And the angel said to her,
"Do not be afraid, Mary, for you have found favour with God

*And behold, you will conceive in your womb and **bear a son**, and you shall **call his name** Jesus.*

> Mary is a virgin, (that is, she is betrothed but not yet married). And this apparition tells her that she will conceive and have a son. He even tells her what to name this son! He may be on a diplomatic mission from God, but he is no diplomat. What about what Mary wants for her life? But there is more! The angel goes on:

He will be great, and will be called the Son of the Most High; and the Lord God will give to him the throne of his father David,
and he will reign over the house of Jacob for ever; and of his kingdom there will be no end."

> At twelve or thirteen years of age how does one deal with such a sudden overwhelming message? How can she conceive since she is not yet married? Mary is very confused. Is this a foretelling? Or, a command? Or, an offer? Or what? How could a son of hers who was a lowly handmaid such as her be a king? The royal throne of King David! For a boy from Nazareth?
> Anyway, hasn't she vowed to remain a virgin for her lifetime?

And Mary said to the angel,
"How shall this be, since I do not know a man?"

> And she expresses her confusion. Mary does not seem to think that this is a foretelling of something that will happen after she is wed. Is this because it is the intention of her and Joseph that their loving marriage will not be consummated physically?

And the angel said to her,
"The Holy Spirit will come upon you,
and the power of the Most High will overshadow you;

> An allusion to the overshadowing by God of the Ark of the Covenant in Mosaic times. Mary is the new Ark of the new Covenant – the "*God Bearer*".
> **Theotokos**

therefore the child to be born will be called holy,
the Son of God.
And behold, your kinswoman Elizabeth in her old age has also conceived a son;
and this is the sixth month with her who was called barren.
For with God nothing will be impossible."

> Does that mean that Mary can conceive a child while remaining a virgin?
> Is it possible that as foretold by Isaiah:
> *Behold, a young virgin shall conceive and bear a son, and shall call his name Immanuel.*
> In true humility Mary accepts that
> **"with God nothing will be impossible."**

And Mary said,
    "Behold, I am the handmaid of the Lord; let it be to me according to your word."
    And the angel departed from her.

> To use a modern expression this is a "*bombshell*". How can she explain to her parents? What about Joseph? Would anybody believe her? Obviously, Elizabeth did when she said:
> *Blessed are you among women, and blessed is the fruit of your womb! And why is this granted me, that the mother of my Lord should come to me?*

Note:
The Hebrew word "*Immanuel*" means "*God with us*".
The Hebrew word "*Jesus*" means "*God saves*".
It seems that Mary and Joseph remained betrothed but not married, at least not in the physical sense.
*Joseph also went up to Bethlehem to be enrolled with Mary, his **betrothed**, who was with child. And while they were there, the time came for her to be delivered. And she gave birth to her first-born son.*
[I am puzzled as to why Matthew uses the phrase "*first-born son*". Perhaps it is an allusion to the killing of all the first-born at the time of the Passover.]
We are told that:
When his (Jesus') *mother Mary had been **betrothed** to Joseph, before they came together,* (which would be expected to be a year after the date of the betrothal)
she was found to be with child of the Holy Spirit; and (although he did not know at this time who the father was)
*her **husband** Joseph, being a just man and unwilling to put her to shame, resolved to divorce her quietly.*
We are told that an angel informed Joseph that,
that which is conceived in her is of the Holy Spirit
and that Joseph
took his wife, but knew her not until she had borne a son.
The word "*until*" means: up to the time that. No indication is implied as to what may have occurred after the birth. For example, one might say that Francis of Assisi remained a saintly man until he died.
Next, we are told that:
*Joseph also went up to Bethlehem to be enrolled with Mary, his **betrothed**, who was with child. And while they were there, the time came for her to be delivered. And she gave birth to her first-born son.*

This event was about nine months after Joseph had learnt of Mary's pregnancy. They are still betrothed – not married. Several subsequent references contained in the story of the escape to and return from Egypt suggest that Joseph did not marry Mary.

Rise, take the child and his mother, and flee to Egypt...
And he rose and took the child and his mother by night...
Rise, take the child and his mother, and go to the land of Israel...
And he rose and took the child and his mother...

Notice that the phrase used is, *"the child and his mother"*. The reference is to **the** *child*, not **your** *child*.
Also, precedence is given to rescue of *"the child"*.
In similar circumstances one might expect something like, *"take your wife and child"* or, perhaps, *"take your wife and* **the** *child"*.
This seems to indicate that Joseph and Mary did not consummate their marriage – they remained betrothed.

Musings.

How did Mary *"break the news"* to her parents? Did they believe her? It seems probable that they did. But if so, they must have had some assistance from God. Probably not a visit from an angel. More likely a grace similar to that received by Peter when he recognised who Jesus was because
...flesh and blood has not revealed this to you, but my Father who is in heaven.

An angel of the Lord appeared to Joseph in a dream and said, *"Joseph, son of David* [of the Royal House of the Jews]*, do not be afraid to take Mary as your wife, for the child conceived in her is from the Holy Spirit. She will bear a son, and you are to name him Jesus, for he will save his people from their sins."*

But that would have also given him an apprehension of the momentous future course his life would take. He was to be father to the Messiah, a messiah whose life had emanated from God. He was to cherish and instruct the long-awaited Messiah! In what turmoil must his mind have been when he had to escape to Egypt before Herod's massacre of babies; and when he lost 12-year-old Jesus following a visit to the Temple?

Excerpts from Pope Francis' Apostolic Letter.
The greatness of Saint Joseph is that he was the spouse of Mary and the father of Jesus. In this way, he placed himself "at the service of the entire plan of salvation".
Saint Joseph reminds us that those who appear hidden or in the shadows can play an incomparable role in the history of salvation.

Joseph was an extraordinary **ordinary** person!

[Joseph is the patron saint of the Universal Church.
He is also the patron saint of families, fathers, pregnant women, travellers, immigrants, house sellers and buyers, craftsmen, engineers, and
working people in general.]

Tradition.

One Catholic tradition holds that Joseph died peacefully in the presence of Jesus and Mary. According to this tradition, Joseph passed away when Jesus was an adolescent, likely in 18 or 19 AD, which is the time of *"Joseph when Jesus died"*, indicating that he died before Jesus' public ministry began. St. Epiphanius gives him ninety years of age at the time of his demise; and if we are to believe the Venerable Bede, he was buried in the Valley of Josaphat.

[Note: I don't think that he was 90 years old when he died – more like 50 years old!]

Joseph and Mary.
[*The great love story*]

Could it be that, apart from God's love for us:

the story of Joseph and Mary is the greatest love story in history?

Who was Joseph?
The gospel of Matthew gives a genealogy for Joseph that is different from that given by Luke. These are the final parts of the lists of Joseph's ancestors:

Matthew	Luke
Azor	Mattathias
Zadok	Joseph
Achim	Jannai
Eliud	Melchi
Eleazar	Levi
Matthan	Matthat
Jacob	**Heli**
Joseph	*Joseph*

So, was Joseph's father Jacob or Heli?

St. Augustine proposed that one line is that of Joseph's biological father and one is of his adoptive father. Brant Pitre in his talk on *"The Jewish Roots of St. Joseph"* tends to agree and suggests that Joseph may (like Jesus) have been an adopted son. As such he would have been eminently suited to nurture an adopted child.

My imagined story begins in Galilee.

Many years before Joseph was born God had made promises to Abraham. His descendants, the Jewish people, would be chosen to be the conduit through whom all the nations of the earth would bless themselves. And so, through Moses, God led his chosen people out of their bondage in Egypt and gave them the land of Israel. The Jews kept themselves separated from all other nations through observation of the commandments given to them. They lived as a separate nation awaiting the coming of the Messiah through the royal Davidic line.

>Joseph *"was of the House of David"*.

Herod the Great (72 BC to 4 BC), had expanded the Second Temple and built other magnificent edifices such as the fortress at Masada and the city of Caesarea Maritima.
His son, Herod Antipas (20 BC to 20AD) had a dream. He would rebuild Sepphoris into the *"Ornament of Galilee"*.

Joseph Bar-Heli was a carpenter and builder. As a young man he had gone from Bethlehem to Sepphoris, a place where there was much work to be had. For part of this time he lodged in Nazareth, about three miles away. It was there that he first set eyes on the young daughter of Joachim and Anne. And she, Mary, set eyes upon him. Love struck each of them like a *coup de foudre* ("*a bolt of lightning*"). Thereafter on each morning on his trek to work I like to think that Joseph might have burst into song:

>*When first I saw the love-light in your eyes*
>*I dreamed the world held naught but joy for me.*
>*And even while we are apart*

I never dream but what I dream of thee.

I love you as I never loved before
since first I saw you on the village green.
Come to me or my dream of love is o'er.
I love you as I loved you, when you were sweet,
when you were sweet thirteen.

Their great desire was to live their lives together as husband and wife. But there was a problem. Well, two problems. Mary had taken a solemn vow to remain a virgin for her life and dedicate herself to God (how little she knew of how wholly and gloriously this commitment would be realised!).

The Old Testament recognised that women, whether single, married or widowed could take an oath to remain virginal.

So, while she was prepared to marry Joseph, they could not have sexual relations.

That Mary remained a virgin for life is explicated in Brant Pitre's book, "*Jesus and the Jewish roots of Mary*".

Could it be that Joseph so wanted to live the rest of his life with Mary that he was happy to forego the joy of sexual love to honour her commitment to God? Yes.

And could it be that Mary so wanted to spend the rest of her life with Joseph that she was happy to accept that he would honour her vow? Yes.

I think so. But of course, this was not the love story that the evangelists set out to write.

Joseph was happy to honour Mary's vow of virginity. But there was a second problem. What about an heir? Joseph as the reigning (although secretly for fear of the Roman overlords) Davidic king of the Jews would be expected to produce an heir to the throne. Well, it seems that Joseph decided that the Davidic line could be continued through another family line as had previously happened in the line of the dynasty.

And so, Joseph and Mary were betrothed.
And Joseph began building a house for them in Nazareth.
That Spring while they were living apart something stupendous happened.
Unbeknownst to Joseph Mary had a visit from an angel and agreed to become the mother of the Son of God.
She became pregnant.
Poor idealistic Joseph – his world fell apart.
When Mary had been betrothed to Joseph, before they came together, she was found to be with child; and her husband Joseph, being a just man and unwilling to put her to shame, resolved to divorce her quietly.

Joseph was so deeply in love with Mary that he wanted to live with her while honouring her vow of virginity and was happy to do so. They had become betrothed to one another. For Joseph life must have been blissful. And now he learns that she is pregnant! What a devastating shock. (It seems that Mary did not tell him about Gabriel's visit). And he knows that he is not the father. He trusted Mary without reservation. Joseph's world is completely shattered.

But as he considered this, behold, an angel of the Lord appeared to him in a dream, saying, "Joseph, son of David, do not fear to take Mary your wife, for that which is conceived in her is of the Holy Spirit; she will bear a son, and you shall call his name Jesus, for he will save his people from their sins."

What did Joseph make of this? Well for a start he believed and took Mary as his wife. He realised that the prophesy of Isaiah:
> *Behold, a young woman shall conceive and bear a son,*
> *and shall call his name Immanuel*

had been fulfilled in Mary.

As an aside it may be noted that he would fulfil his royal obligation to produce an heir by adopting Jesus, and would fulfil it beyond his greatest imagination. Mary told him of the visit by the angel of God who had proclaimed that:
> *the Lord God will give to him the throne of his father David,*
> *and he will reign over the house of Jacob for ever;*
> *and of his kingdom there will be no end.*

But he would also be aware of an enormous responsibility placed on his shoulders.

And what of the neighbours? When, three months later Mary returned from her visit to Elizabeth, everybody would soon become aware that Mary was pregnant and know that the wedding (which usually took place a year after the betrothal) had not taken place. Having regard to what was to happen in December it seems that Mary moved in to Joseph's house and they lived, to all outward appearances, as husband and wife.

Then prophesies are fulfilled.

> *But you, O **Bethlehem** Ephrathah,*
> *who are little to be among the clans of Judah,*
> *from you shall come forth for me*
> *one who is to be ruler in Israel,*

> *whose origin is from of old,*
> *from ancient days.*
>
> Micah 5:2.
>
> *Therefore, the Lord himself will give you a sign. Behold, a young woman shall conceive and bear a son, and shall call his name Immanuel.*
>
> Isaiah 7:14.

Mary was coming to the end of her pregnancy when *a decree went out from Caesar Augustus that all the world should be enrolled... And all went to be enrolled, each to his own city. And Joseph also went up from Galilee, from the city of Nazareth, to Judea, to the city of David, which is called Bethlehem, because he was of the house and lineage of David, to be enrolled with Mary, his betrothed, who was with child. And while they were there, the time came for her to be delivered. And she gave birth to her first-born son and wrapped him in swaddling clothes, and laid him in a manger, because there was no place for them in the inn.*

What a journey (about 90 miles) to have to make when in the last days of one's pregnancy. Isn't it strange that the prophesy of Micah was fulfilled 700 years later because of the edict of a pagan emperor?

Mary and Joseph were faithfully observant of the Mosaic Law as was Jesus throughout his life. They brought Jesus to the Temple to be circumcised and later, when they visited the Temple for Mary's Purification they met a prophet and a prophetess. He spoke of Jesus as *a light for revelation to the Gentiles, and for glory to thy people Israel* and *she gave thanks to God, and spoke of him to all who were looking for the redemption of Jerusalem.*

Many came to visit the newly born child including three men from the East. Now, Herod had learned from these men that they were on their way to visit *he who has been born king of the Jews*. Herod, who was a puppet king became very alarmed to think that there might be a legitimate Jewish king and, on being informed by the chief priests and scribes of Micah's prophesy determined to get rid of this threat to his kingship. He had asked the wise men from the East to let him know where the new king was. But they were warned by an angel to bypass Herod. When, after some time, he realised the wise men were not coming back to hum, Herod *killed all the male children in Bethlehem and in all that region who were two years old or under*. What a monster.

But, *an angel of the Lord had appeared to Joseph in a dream and said, "Rise, take the child and his mother, and flee to Egypt, and remain there till I tell you; for Herod is about to search for the child, to destroy him." And he rose and took the child and his mother by night, and departed to Egypt.* This would have been a long and arduous journey for a young mother and infant child. Depending on where in Egypt they went the journey would have taken at least a week.

When Herod died, behold, an angel of the Lord appeared in a dream to Joseph in Egypt, saying, "Rise, take the child and his mother, and go to the land of Israel, for those who sought the child's life are dead." And he rose and took the child and his mother, and went to the land of Israel. But when he heard that Archelaus reigned over Judea in place of his father Herod, he was afraid to go there, and being warned in a dream he withdrew to the district of Galilee. And he went and dwelt in a city called Nazareth, that what was spoken by the prophets might be fulfilled, "He shall be called a Nazarene."

It is breathtaking to see that God chose Joseph (a labourer) rather than a learned scribe or Pharisee (such as Gamaliel) to instruct his Son in the Jewish religion and the Law and the Prophets. And to prepare him to be the Messiah!

Judging from what Jesus is reported as teaching in the gospels he seems to have done a good job – Jesus' talks are rife with Old Testament allusions.

On the way home from one of their annual visits to Jerusalem his parents discovered that Jesus was not with their caravan. They must have been in a dreadful state of mind until they found him three days later. He was in the Temple *sitting among the teachers, listening to them and asking them questions.* He was only twelve years old! Yet, *all who heard him were amazed at his understanding and his answers.*

He went down with them to Nazareth, and was obedient to them. Mary kept all these things in her heart. And Jesus increased in wisdom and in stature, and in favour with God and man.

We hear no more of Joseph. I like to think that he lived joyfully with his beloved and with his son for many years and did not die until a few years before the wedding feast at Cana.

Historical note:

In biblical times, people were married in early youth, and marriages were usually contracted within the narrow circle of the clan and the family. It was undesirable to marry a woman from a foreign clan, lest she introduce foreign beliefs and practices. As a rule, the fathers arranged the match. The girl was consulted, but the *"calling of the damsel and inquiring at her mouth"* after the conclusion of all negotiations was merely a formality. Did Joseph's adoptive father and Mary's father arrange their match? If Mary had taken a vow to remain a virgin for her life why would any match be arranged?

Marriage consisted of two ceremonies that were marked by celebrations at two separate times, with an interval between.

First came the betrothal [*erusin*]; and later, the wedding [*nissuin*]. A betrothal was more than simply an engagement as we understand it today. At the betrothal the man and woman were legally married, although she still remained a virgin in her father's house. The wedding meant only that the betrothed woman, accompanied by a colourful procession, was brought from her father's house to the house of her groom, and the legal tie with him was to be consummated.

In those days the betrothal was the more important of these two events and maintained its importance as long as marriage was actually based upon a purchase. But as women assumed more importance as individuals, and marriage ceased to be a purchase, attaining moral significance, the actual wedding became more important than the betrothal.

The man with "*great possessions*".
[*Mark10:17-22*]

And as he was setting out on his journey, a man ran up and knelt before him, and asked him,
"*Good Teacher, what must I do to inherit eternal life?*"
And Jesus was very pleased to meet a man who believed in life after death – one who wished to inherit or be given eternal life. One who might recognise Jesus as the Divine Messiah. And, looking on him and loving him, said to him,
"*Why do you call me Good?*"
And then there was a long pause as Jesus looked deeply into the man's eyes. He hoped that the man would reflect on why he called Jesus "*Good*". Could he not see that the numerous miracles wrought by Jesus and particularly the forgiving of sins were signs pointing to his divinity? Would he see that the sayings of Jesus were pointers to his fulfilment of the Law and the Prophets?
Time passed.
Then Jesus gave him a further nudge:
"*No one is Good but God alone.*"
The implication being: if you think that I am Good, then since only God can be Good, don't you know why you call me Good?
Time passed.
As the man did not respond Jesus did not pursue the matter any further and said to him:
"*You know the commandments…keep these.*"
The man assured Jesus that he had always kept the commandments.
Jesus, hoping that the man could in time recognise Who Jesus was invited him to
"*…go, sell what you have, and give to the poor…*
and come, follow me."

But the man could not do that. Well, not at that moment.
Might he have seen the light at some later time? Who knows?

Such a sad story.
What would I have done?

Jesus curses the fig tree.

On the following day [Holy Monday], *when they came from Bethany, he was hungry. And seeing in the distance a fig tree in leaf, he went to see if he could find anything on it. When he came to it, he found nothing but leaves, for it was not the season for figs. And he said to it, "May no one ever eat fruit from you again." And his disciples heard it.*

Mark 11:12-14.

As they passed by in the morning [Holy Tuesday], *they saw the fig tree withered away to its root. And Peter remembered and said to him, "Master, look! The fig tree which you cursed has withered. And Jesus answered them, "Have faith in God".*

Mark 11:20-22.

I have always been puzzled by this account. This took place in the springtime when, as the story points out, *it was not the season for figs.* And, even more puzzlingly, why would the evangelist report on such a matter? What could this have to do with bringing us the Good News? Jesus, being who he was, could not have been suffering from the "*Monday morning blues*". Brant Pitre suggests that Jesus' action was figurative and intended to throw one's mind back to the Fall of Adam and Eve. They sinned by eating the forbidden fruit of the "*tree of knowledge of good and evil*". Due to many pictures of that moment we tend to think of that fruit as an apple. That was not what the ancient Jews thought. They thought of the tree as a fig tree. The apocryphal book, *Life of Adam and Eve* contains the following:

[Eve said:] *At that very moment my eyes were opened, and I knew that I was naked of the righteousness with which I had been clothed... 1 looked for leaves... so that I might cover my shame, but I did not find (any) from the trees of Paradise... except (those) of the fig tree only. And I took its leaves and made for myself skirts; they were from the same plants of which I ate.*

So, at the beginning of Holy Week, Jesus was figuratively destroying the allegorical source of evil in the world before going on to actually overcome the satanic source in his passion, death, resurrection and ascension.

Healing the woman with the haemorrhage.
[*Mark 5:25-34*]

And a great crowd followed him and thronged about him. And there was a woman who had had a flow of blood for twelve years, and who had suffered much under many physicians, and had spent all that she had, and was no better but rather grew worse.
She had heard the reports about Jesus,
and came up behind him in the crowd and touched his garment. For she said,
"*If I touch even his garments, I shall be made well.*"
And immediately the haemorrhage ceased; and she felt in her body that she was healed of her disease.

And Jesus, perceiving in himself that power had gone forth from him, immediately turned about in the crowd, and said,
"*Who touched my garments?*"
And his disciples said to him,
"*You see the crowd pressing around you, and yet you say, 'Who touched me?'*"
And he looked around to see who had done it.

But the woman, knowing what had been done to her, came in fear and trembling and fell down before him, and told him the whole truth.
And he said to her,
"Daughter, your faith has made you well; go in peace, and be healed of your disease."

This woman has great faith in Yeshua – she does not need to ask him to cure her – she does not even have to be touched by him – she does not even face him ("*she came up behind him in the crowd*") – nobody in the crowd would know what had happened with her.

We are told that Yeshua, *perceived in himself that power had gone forth from him*. Well, of course we know that Yeshua would perceive this and that the power would not have been exercised unless he wished it to be. So, as we might say in Dublin:

> "*Why would he make a public show of her?*"
> "*Why not save her blushes.*"
> "*Why not let her get on with her life.*"

Could it be that Yeshua was seeking applause? Was it because, while he *perceived in himself that power had gone forth from him*, he didn't know what had happened as a result? Did he wish to embarrass the poor woman?

I don't think so.

This woman had suffered for twelve years. In the eyes of her people she was ritually impure. She could not go into the Temple. Anything she touched or anybody who touched her would become unclean or impure. Thus, she would have been an outcast for twelve years and well known in the town.

It seems apparent from the description of the crowds thronging around him that Yeshua was held in high esteem by the townspeople. So, what Yeshua did was not to expose her to embarrassment. It was to proclaim that the woman was no longer unclean and free to enter the Temple and mix with her neighbours.

If he hadn't done this, who would have believed her to be unclean because of an alleged unseen touch of Yeshua's garment? Now, perhaps she was perceived as "*special*"!

This event seems to have been widely proclaimed because later (Mark:6-56) we are told:

*And wherever he came, in villages, cities, or country, they... besought him that they might **touch even the fringe of his garment;***
and as many as touched it were made well.

Phenomenal Acclaim.

It may be somewhat irreverential to say it, but isn't this the kind of thing that happens to pop stars? Remember the more than five thousand and the more than four thousand who followed him into the countryside? There were probably several other similar gatherings during Jesus' three-year ministry which are not recorded in the gospels. It seems to me that because *"the harvest was plentiful, but the labourers were few"* Jesus knew that more ministers than the twelve apostles were needed for the Church that he was establishing.

The establishment of the Christian Church.

The Apostles. *Bishops?*
And he called to him his twelve disciples and gave them authority over unclean spirits, to cast them out, and to heal every disease and every infirmity. Matthew 10:1

The harvest was indeed plentiful. More labourers were needed. So, Jesus turned to his disciples and he said to one, *"Follow me."* But he said, *"Lord, **let me first** go and bury my father."* But he said to him, *"Leave the dead to bury their own dead; but as for you, go and proclaim the kingdom of God."* Another said, *"I will follow you, Lord; **but let me first** say farewell to those at my home."* Jesus said to him, *"No one who puts his hand to the plough and looks back is fit for the kingdom of God."*

Jesus needed dedicated ministers and so:

The appointees. *Priests?*
After this the Lord **appointed seventy others**, and sent them on ahead of him, **two by two**, into every town and place **where he himself was about to come**. And he said to them, whenever you enter a town…say to them, ***"The kingdom of God has come near to you."*** Luke 10:1-16.

Jesus had planned his mission. It seems that he intended to visit at least thirty-six towns and villages in and around Galilee. He would start in Galilee.

Galilee was not a large area but, due to its fertile soil, particularly in Lower Galilee, it was densely inhabited. Compare:

	Area Square miles	Population	Persons per square mile
Galilee	1,350	400,000	300
Wicklow	1,215	114,700	95

It was roughly the same size as Wicklow but more crowded. It was hemmed in on all sides by hostile neighbours.

There were four cities (including Sepphoris) with populations up to 50,000 in each.

There were about 300 towns and villages in Galilee with populations ranging up to 1,000 persons.

A note from Monsignor Charles Pope

The average village in Galilee might be no more than a few acres with a population of a few hundred souls.

The world was pretty much limited to their small village and the fields around it. The inhabitants lived in modest one-story houses of stone covered with a kind of stucco.

The houses tended to be clustered around a town square. In the square were some shops, an open air market, and usually a communal well or spring.

Each town had a handful of local craftsman, typically including a potter, a weaver, a carpenter, a blacksmith, and a shoemaker. Most of the men in the village, however, worked in the fields, whether tilling, sowing, pruning, or harvesting. Life was a long, difficult struggle against the elements.

Most families kept a small number of animals such as sheep and goats. These were useful for milk, wool, and eventually leather and food. Most villages also had a shepherd or two tending village flocks on the nearby hillsides.

On many evenings the men gathered in the village synagogue for evening services and Scripture study. During the day the synagogue served as a school for the young men of the village, who learned ancient Hebrew and studied the Scriptures. Most people no longer spoke Hebrew; it was a sacred language used only in the Temple and in the synagogue, similar to Latin for the Catholic Church. Most villagers spoke Aramaic, but they also knew some Greek because it was the native tongue of the pagans around them. The Jews of Galilee spoke with a distinctive accent.

Villages were often in well-protected locations. They were generally built on hilltops rather than in the long sloping valleys. Here they were more easily protected and the best land in the valleys was reserved for agriculture.

The streets were generally quite narrow, more like alleys. The homes that fronted the streets came right up to the edge of the street. The walls of homes tended to be at least ten feet high, with only a few windows at the top. This is because one generally entered a home by walking into an open courtyard off the street. Whereas we tend to have front yards today, homes at this time tended to have courtyards, around which were clustered rooms of varying size depending on the wealth and needs of the owner.

Villages tended to be small because the needs of each village were associated with pastureland around it. Each village depended on both crops and the livestock that used the surrounding fields and the sloping valley beneath. Further, each village was either built around or near a well or spring.

Each village tended to be self-sustaining in terms of basic needs. Occasionally, people would come from larger towns to provide specialized services, but except for a yearly pilgrimage, most Galileans did not travel far from their village.

Nazareth was a fairly typical Galilean village. It was laid out on a steep hillside and at the time of Jesus probably had no more than 300 residents.

This is the *milieu* into which the thirty-five groups appointed by Jesus first ventured to prepare people for the Good News that the Kingdom of God had come near to them.

The number of people following Jesus had grown at a great rate as is somewhat incidentally mentioned by Luke.

After his baptism and his 40 days in the desert Jesus returned in the power of the Spirit into **Galilee**, *and a report concerning him went out through* **all the surrounding country.** *And he taught in their synagogues, being glorified by all.*

But then:
he came to **Nazareth**, *where he had been brought up; and he went to the synagogue, as his custom was, on the sabbath day. And he stood up to read… and all spoke well of him, and wondered at the gracious words which proceeded out of his mouth…*
but then
they rose up and put him out of the city.
"*A prophet is not without honour, except in his hometown and among his relatives and in his own household.*"

And he went down to **Capernaum** and in the synagogue
*a man who had the spirit of an unclean demon cried out
"What have you to do with us, Jesus of Nazareth? I know who
you are, the Holy One of God."*
**And reports of him went out into every place in the
surrounding region.**
*And the people sought him and came to him, and would have
kept him from leaving them*
but he went to preach the good news of the kingdom of God
to the other cities also.

*And he was preaching in the synagogues of **Judea**.
Jesus called Simon, Andrew, James and John.
As he was teaching, there were **Pharisees and teachers of the
law** sitting by, who had come from every village of Galilee
and Judea and from Jerusalem.*

Jesus' teachings, unlike those of the Pharisees and scribes,
were positive and resonated with the ordinary people. The
establishment could see its power over the people dissipating
while more and more people turned to Jesus.
*And the scribes and the Pharisees began to question, saying,
"Who is this that speaks blasphemies? Who can forgive sins
but God only?"*

*In these days he went out to the mountain to pray...and he
called his disciples, and chose from them **twelve**, whom he
named **apostles**.
And he came down with them and stood on a level place, with
a great crowd of his disciples and a **great multitude of people
from all Judea and Jerusalem and the seacoast of Tyre and
Sidon**.
And when a great crowd came together and people from*

town after town came to him…

The apostles had been with Jesus on his journeys but, by now the number of people following Jesus had grown too many for him to talk with on his own.
And he called the twelve together…and he sent them out to preach the kingdom of God and to heal.

Jesus feeds five thousand. Jesus feeds four thousand.

The Transfiguration

And the number of followers continued to grow and so:
The Lord appointed seventy others, and sent them on ahead of him, two by two, into every town and place where he himself was about to come.

Jesus Denounces Pharisees and Lawyers
Being asked by the Pharisees when the kingdom of God was coming, he answered them, "behold, the kingdom of God is in the midst of you."

Initially the lawyers sought to confound Jesus by reference to his understanding of the Law and the Prophets.
And he was teaching daily in the Temple [Now he is at the core of the establishment!]. *The chief priests and the scribes and the principal men of the people sought to destroy him; but they did not find anything they could do, for all the people hung upon his words.*

But Jesus exposed their misunderstanding of God's word.
The scribes and the chief priests tried to lay hands on him at that very hour, but they feared the people; for they perceived

that he had told this parable against them. So, they watched him, and sent spies, who pretended to be sincere, that they might take hold of what he said, so as to deliver him up to the authority and jurisdiction of the governor.

Some may have believed in Jesus.
And some of the scribes answered, "Teacher, you have spoken well." For they no longer dared to ask him any question. And the chief priests and the scribes were seeking how to put him to death; for they feared the people.

The final *"straws"*:
                    Jesus raises Lazarus to life.

A very large crowd spread their cloaks on the road, and others cut branches from the trees and spread them on the road. The crowds that went ahead of him and that followed were shouting,
        "Hosanna to the Son of David!
Blessed is the one who comes in the name of the Lord!
Hosanna in the highest heaven!"
When he entered Jerusalem, **the whole city was in turmoil***, asking, "Who is this?" The crowds were saying,*
    "This is the prophet Jesus from Nazareth in Galilee."

The world is a mess – is there hope?

- The Bible tells us that before anything existed there was a Being whom we call "*God*". There were no spirits, no space, no matter and there was no such thing as time.
- And this God was all perfect and needing nothing.
  - So, why did God create anything?
  - Why did God create me?
  - Why did God allow evil?
- Our Catholic Church teaches us that, while there is One God, there are three Persons in this One God.
- Excerpts from Catechism of the Catholic Church 295 – 314:
  - God freely created the world according to his wisdom – he wanted to make his creatures share in his being, wisdom and goodness;
  - God created freely "*out of nothing*";
  - God's creation is ordered.
  - God's creation is good: "*And God saw everything that he had made, and behold, it was very good.*";
  - God transcends creation and is present to it.
  - God upholds and sustains creation.
  - Divine Providence. Creation has its own goodness and proper perfection, but it did not spring forth complete from the hands of the Creator. The universe was created "*in a state of journeying*" toward an ultimate perfection yet to be attained, to which God has destined it. We call "*divine providence*" the dispositions by which God guides his creation towards this perfection.
  - To human beings God even gives the power of freely sharing in his providence by entrusting them

with the responsibility of *"subduing the earth and having dominion over it"*.
- God created the universe – space, time and matter/energy. Most of us are somewhat familiar with the accounts of the days of creation related in Genesis. It is interesting to compare this account with the modern Big Bang theory. Author Brian Swimme provides us with a brief layman's guide in his reader-friendly book and here is a brief extract:

Extract from *"Journey of the Universe"*.

Let's begin at the very beginning. How did it all start? An awesome question, certainly, but it appears there really was a beginning. Some scientists refer to this as the Big Bang. Let's think of it as a great flaring forth of light and matter, both the luminous matter that would eventually become stars and galaxies and the dark matter that no one has ever seen. All of space and time and mass and energy began as a single point that was trillions of degrees hot and that instantly rushed apart.

In the beginning, the universe brought forth quarks and leptons, the elementary particles, and within a few microseconds the quarks combined to form protons and neutrons that churned ceaselessly in a thick and gluey form of matter called plasma. There was almost no structure in the universe. These quanta would collide, would interact with one another, and then would scatter apart to collide with different partners millions of times each instant.

But there is another fundamental force at play in our universe: a force of attraction, pulling things together—a force we call gravity. The universe expanded and cooled, and gravity pulled some of the matter together to form the galaxies and stars. These two opposing dynamics, expansion and contraction, were the dominant powers operating at the beginning of the universe.

One of the most spectacular features of the observable universe is the elegance of its expansion. If the rate of expansion had been slower, even slightly slower, even one millionth of a percent slower, the universe would have recollapsed. It would have imploded upon itself, and that would have been the end of the story. Conversely, if the universe had expanded a little more quickly, even one millionth of one percent more quickly, the universe would have expanded too quickly for structures to form. It would have simply diffused into dust, with no structures to bring forth life.[5]

- Is there a conflict between the scientists' account of creation and of evolution and the first three chapters of Genesis? Perhaps. As Catholics we believe the Genesis account to be true because we believe that what was written was inspired by God. What should give us pause for thought is that theologians have been debating the meaning of the Genesis account for the past three thousand five hundred years!
- Astronomers tell us that there are over two billion galaxies and that on average each galaxy has two billion planets. And that that takes up only about five percent of the universe – the rest is Dark Matter and Dark energy.

---

[5] Swimme, Brian Thomas; Tucker, Mary Evelyn. Journey of the Universe. Yale University Press.

- The planet Earth is for us humans. What billions and billions of other planets be for? some kind of gigantic lottery going on for over 14 billion years before achieving the combination giving rise to the planet Earth some four and a half billion years ago?
- Anyway, it seems that the first humans came into being about two or three hundred thousand years ago.
  God created humans in his image, male and female. and said to them, "Be fruitful and multiply and fill the earth and subdue it"
- At this moment in time *God saw everything that he had made, and indeed, it was very good.*
- The *very good* humans have the ability to think and free will. The first humans as described in Genesis seem to have been somewhat aimless. I wonder whether they may have been bored. How might such beings be part of God's plan? Why give us free will?
- Then, *Satan demanded to have humans that he might sift them like wheat.* For some reason known to Himself God permitted this.
- The first couple "*made a bags of it*" and life became difficult.
- And generation after generation became much worse than them to the extent that there was only one decent family on Earth. So, God flooded the Earth and nobody except Noah and his family survived.
- Eventually around 1,800 BC, God chose Abraham and his tribe to be the conduit through which he would be revealed to all mankind. They prospered for a time but then moved to a pagan country and became enslaved for four hundred years until they were rescued and given

to live and led into a new country which
1.

ospered for a while until they were
veral times and many were scattered to
es.

as in a mess again. What to do? God had
with Noah to never again destroy mankind
and ... braham that he would give him a land, numerous descendants, his blessing and, through Abraham, his blessing of all nations. God would now intervene through his Son.
- So, God became a man (named Jesus), modified the Mosaic rules, explained how humans could live eternally with God, was executed, rose from the dead and ascended into heaven. He allowed us to continue to make him present daily under the appearance of bread, appointed a leader (a kind of prime minister) and sent another Person of God to guide us spiritually.
- One might be tempted to wonder if this was in vain since, the more that mankind prospered and learned about *"how things work"*, the more men escalated methods of mutually destructive warfare culminating in today's monumental absurdity where:
  - Detonating about 400 atomic bombs would be sufficient to wipe out humanity.
  - And yet, the world's nuclear-armed states possess a combined total of about 12,000 nuclear warheads, that is 30 times as many as are needed to destroy humanity.
- Perhaps we will be spared nuclear extermination. Scientists tell us that the planet is overheating causing many destructive effects. Maybe we will be culled by a reaction from Nature: rising temperatures, bad air, crop

failures, malevolent covid-like epidemics. But some will survive – remember the Noahic covenant when God promised that *that never again shall all flesh be cut off by the waters of a flood, and never again shall there be a flood to destroy the earth.* But ninety nine percent is not "*all*".

- Today's golden calves are money and sexual promiscuity.
- According to Oxfam the richest 1 percent have more wealth than the bottom 95 percent of the world's population.
- Satan is rampant:
    - Money has replaced God as the end to be sought;
    - The day of rest has ceased to be such;
    - Christmas, the day on which the Word was made flesh, has been supplanted by Santa Claus;
    - The Easter Resurrection has been supplanted by chocolate eggs; and
    - The world is full of noise 24/7.
    - The "*now*" is kidnapped and drowned in noise.
- At the present time harmony is missing. Too many notes in the symphony of the story of humankind are raucous and many notes are subdued. So many of the Composer's human assistants are not in tune with his music.
- In the 1961 census in Ireland 95% of us identified as Catholic; in 2016 79% identified as Catholic; in 2022 69% identified. These are statistics from a census. When one compares church attendance in the 1960's (churches overflowed each Sunday) with church attendance today one suspects that the percentage is a good deal lower. We have public figures alleging that the Catholic Church is a "*spent force*" and even that it is "*a force for evil*". Is Satan winning?

- I think that the problematic situation in which we find ourselves goes back to the time of Constantine when in the year 313 he proclaimed freedom of practice for the Christian religion. Then in 380 Theodosius II proclaimed Christianity to be the State religion. This would have appeared to be stupendously good news for the church. Unfortunately, the church then adopted the State methodology of control and Law rather than living as an attraction to the Good News. An error similar to that of the Jews who chose the Law rather than the Prophets.
- Jesus came to fulfil the Law and the Prophets through righteousness and adherence to the *"greatest commandments"* given to the Jews 1,200 years previously:
  > *Hear, O Israel: The Lord our God is one Lord; and you shall love the Lord your God with all your heart, and with all your soul, and with all your might.*
  >
  >   Deuteronomy 6:4-5.
  > *You shall not hate your brother in your heart, but you shall reason with your neighbour, lest you bear sin because of him. You shall not take vengeance or bear any grudge against the sons of your own people,* **but you shall love your neighbour as yourself:** *I am the Lord.*
  >
  >   Leviticus 19:17-18.
- These *"commandments"* were endorsed by Jesus as the *"first of all"* – Mark 12:29-31.
- Simply put: the Mosaic commandments are based on the Natural Law and are to be observed governed and inspired by love of God (the Creator of all) and love of our fellow humans (created in the image and likeness of God).

- The Church should spread the *Good News* through attraction to the Christian way of living rather than through control of members of its body.
- "Commandments" and "rules" are needed for initial guidance – they are basic *aide memoires*. Even if God did not have Moses carve on stone *"Thou shalt not kill"*, we would know that killing someone would be wrong – a breach of the Natural Law – a sin.
- One only needs to read a newspaper, turn on the TV or look around to see that these Commandments – ALL of them - are being broken every minute of every day throughout our world.
- It might seem that Satan is having his way. Remember that, with Judas, he even managed to get in for part of the Last Supper!
- We are told that today there are about 1.3 billion Catholics in a world population of about 8 billion – that's about 16% of us.
- My mind goes back to a defining moment in Jesus' ministry as recounted in John 6. The five thousand who had been fed with five loaves and two fish followed him to Capernaum. When Jesus told them that they must eat his body and drink his blood to have life they *disputed among themselves, saying, "How can this man give us his flesh to eat?" After this many of his disciples drew back and no longer went about with him.* They did not believe that he was *the Son of man on whom God the Father has set his seal*.
- Because of this unbelief, they did not believe, as Mary had that,
  "with God nothing will be impossible."
- Peter, although puzzled and perplexed, did believe and when asked if he would leave Jesus replied,

Lord, to whom shall we go? You have the words of eternal life; and we have believed, and have come to know, that you are the Holy One of God.

- At times like the present, we need to have faith like Peter and the apostles and that as Jesus promised,

    ...the powers of death shall not prevail against it [my church]

    because as he also promised,

    I am with you always, to the close of the age.

- And, in the fulness of time,

    *with the clouds of heaven
    there will come* ~~one like a~~ **Son of Man**,
    and he will come to the Ancient of Days [God the Father]
    *and be presented before him.
    And to him is given dominion
    and glory and kingdom,
    that all peoples, nations, and languages
    should serve him;
    his dominion is an everlasting dominion,
    which shall not pass away,
    and his kingdom one
    that shall not be destroyed.*

"with God nothing will be impossible."

PURGATORY or, the final purification.

The Catechism of the Catholic Church teaches us that:
*All who die in God's grace and friendship, but still imperfectly **purified**, are indeed assured of their eternal salvation; but after death they **undergo purification**, so as to achieve the holiness necessary to enter the joy of heaven.*
*The Church gives the name Purgatory to this final **purification** of the elect, which is entirely different from the punishment of the damned. The Church formulated her doctrine of faith on Purgatory especially at the Councils of Florence and Trent. The tradition of the Church, by reference to certain texts of Scripture, speaks of **a cleansing fire**: As for certain lesser faults, we must believe that, before the Final Judgment, there is a **purifying** fire…*

The Catechism (336) also asserts that:
*Beside each believer stands an angel as protector and shepherd leading him to **life**.*

In 2007 Pope Benedict XVI in his encyclical on hope (*Spe Salvi*) included the following (abridged by me!):
The early Jewish idea of an intermediate state includes the view that these souls are not simply in a sort of temporary custody but, as the parable of the rich man illustrates, are already being punished or are experiencing a provisional form of bliss. There is also the idea that this state can involve **purification** and healing which **mature the soul for communion with God**…With death, our life-choice becomes definitive—our life stands before the judge…
For the great majority of people…there remains in the depths of their being an ultimate interior openness to truth, to love, to God. In the concrete choices of life, however, it is covered over by ever new compromises with evil—**much filth covers**

purity, but the thirst for purity remains and it still constantly re-emerges from all that is base and remains present in the soul. What happens to such individuals when they appear before the Judge? Will all the impurity they have amassed through life suddenly cease to matter? What else might occur? Saint Paul, in his *First Letter to the Corinthians*…begins by saying that Christian life is built upon a common foundation: Jesus Christ. This foundation endures. If we have stood firm on this foundation and built our life upon it, we know that **it cannot be taken away from us** even in death. Then Paul continues… **we personally have to pass through "fire" so as to become fully open** to receiving God and able to take our place at the table of the eternal marriage-feast.

Some recent theologians are of the opinion that…before the gaze of Christ all falsehood melts away. This encounter with him, as it burns us, transforms and frees us, **allowing us to become truly ourselves**…But it is **a blessed pain**, in which the holy power of his love sears through us like a flame, enabling us to become totally ourselves and thus totally of God…The transforming "moment" of this encounter **eludes earthly time-reckoning**…The judgement of God is hope, both because it is justice and because it is grace. …**grace allows us all to hope**, and to go trustfully to meet the Judge whom we know as our "*advocate*", or *parakletos* (cf. *1 Jn* 2:1).

I used to have a very fuzzy idea of what purgatory might be. I didn't know if were you part of a crowd or solitary in a cell? Apparently you were burnt in a fire for a certain amount of time? But, how could a soul be burned? What would that achieve anyway? It sounded like one was to be tortured (and more so than those in Guantanamo Bay!) until one admitted all of one's sins, accepted full and sole responsibility for them and apologised in a credible and acceptable manner. And then was punished an amount measured to be sufficient penalty. Obviously this scenario was based on how earthly justice systems work. But, after death one will be in a heavenly court where Justice will be administered with Mercy and where grace will prevail.

Now I have a different kind of concept.

The thing we know for sure about death is that my body ceases to work, to be alive, to have life, to have lifeness. I am certain that I am more than my physical body – I can't prove that – call it a feeling if you like. I am *"me"*. I was always *"me"* – before and at birth, at 5 years, at 25 years, at 55 years – always the same essential *"me"*. After death I am still me, but, without integration in my body – unable to use my physical senses. I cannot see, hear or feel anything through my body – I am further removed from sensing communication with the physical world than I would be in sleep or in a coma. I have been told that my soul lives on immortally.

First of all the pain: after death I think that I will develop a much more comprehensive realisation of what the Beatific Vision can be. This will be accompanied by an irrepressible and urgent desire in the most fundamental depth of my heart to be in God's company. And lack of immediate access is where the seemingly never-ending pain will come from – excruciating pining.

What about *"purification"*? Now, what follows may be silly, but it is what I like to imagine.

All my life I have had a guardian angel *to whom God's love has committed me*– he/she knows everything about me, the good and the bad. And that includes subconscious stuff, blind spots and dreams. He/she is devoted to me *"to light and guard, to rule and guide"*. St. Augustine reckoned that *angels are created wisdom, enlightened in their love of God, perfected at the beginning of their creation, always beholding the Father's face. As perfected intellectual spirits, angels possess a knowledge of creation in God that allows them to oversee all of creation.*

I don't think that my guardian angel will abandon me when I die. I reckon that he is committed to endeavouring to guide me to our maker. Having chaperoned me on Earth, he will accompany me to some kind of antechamber where he will counsel me and then educate me in Truth. I hope and think that he/she will purify me by *"guiding me into the full truth"* and then usher me into heaven. Anyway, that is what I hope. After all, God will be looking on. What would he want? A crushed and cowed survivor or a person who is now more properly

"a human in his image according to his likeness"?

So, yes there will be pain. But it will not be in vain. There will be purifying that will bring me to

What no eye has seen, nor ear heard,
nor the human heart conceived,
which God has prepared for those who love him.

And, to close, some difficult questions.

- Before *"the beginning"*, that is, before the creation of space, time and the universe there was only God. God was perfect and complete in himself and did not need anything. Why would God create humans? Many will say that it was because of an overflowing of love but that doesn't feel to me like the whole reason. So, why?
- Adam and Eve sinned and everything changed. They (and the planet Earth) were punished. Could God have simply forgiven them? I think that the answer is *"yes"*. Why didn't he? Why didn't the Son of Man come on Earth sooner and we could have avoided all that trouble with the generations to Noah, and Abraham's descendants?
- When Jesus did come and fulfil the Law and the Prophets and show us the way, the truth and the life why did he have to suffer such a terrible scourging and death? Thomas Aquinas seems to vacillate on this question. *"No, he didn't"* because **"with God nothing will be impossible"** and *"yes, he did"* because God, being outside time, knew that he would! This is beyond me – my simple approach is that due to the shallowness of somebody like me he had to go to such lengths to demonstrate the depth of his love for us.
- In his letter to the Galatians St. Paul tells us:
"But when the fullness of the time had come, God sent forth His Son, born of a woman, born under the law, to redeem those who were under the law, that we might receive the adoption as sons"
I am aware that Daniel had prophesied that the Messiah would come after 490 years (the fullness of time) but,

why is it the fullness? What is it about the time that Jesus lived that makes it the *fullness of time*? What would the history of mankind have been like if Jesus had come at an earlier or a later time? This is a useless question but I would still like to know how the time at which he came is the *fullness of time*.
- What is certain is that for each of us there will be a *fullness of time*!

Appendix:

The Holy Land – distances.

It was a comparatively small country at about 8,000 square miles. By contrast the province of Ulster is 8,500 square miles.

At its longest it was 290 miles.
At its widest it was 85 miles.

From Nazareth to:	
Cana	4 miles
Capernaum	40 miles
Jerusalem	90 miles
Bethlehem	100 miles
From Capernaum to:	
Bethsaida	6 miles
Magdala	6 miles
Jerusalem	118 miles

Looking west from Jordanian Highlands (4,500 feet high) one can see right across Israel to Mediterranean Sea.

	Sea of Galilee	Lough Neagh	
Length	13 miles	19 miles	6 miles longer
Width	8.1 miles	9.3 miles	1.2 miles wider
Circumference	33 miles	80 miles	47 miles longer
Area	64.4 sq. miles	151 sq. miles	86.6 sq. miles larger
Max. depth	141 feet	80 feet	61 feet

			shallower
Water	Fresh	Fresh	

Place	Area	Population
West bank	2,178 sq. miles	3.2 million
Gaza strip	140 sq. miles	2.0 million
Total	2,310 sq. miles	5.2 million
County Cork	2,899 sq. miles	543,000
Ireland	27,133 sq. miles	5.4 million
Northern Ireland	5,530 sq. miles	1.885 million

Reconstruction of the harbour of Capernaum at the time of Christ, based on archaeological remains. Several piers, which can still be seen when the water level is low, jutted out into the sea to provide a quiet and safe harbour for fishing boats.

Nazareth.

"Can anything good come out of Nazareth?"
[John 1:46.]

Extracts from interview with archaeologist Yardenna Alexandre in The Times of Israel newspaper.

Based on excavated evidence, the tiny, off-the-beaten-path hamlet was inhabited from the Iron Age (10th–8th centuries BCE) onward.

Alexandre discovered the first example of a residential building from the time of Jesus. It was found near today's Church of the Annunciation.

She describes the structure as *"a simple house comprising small rooms and an inner courtyard that was inhabited in the late Hellenistic and the Early Roman periods."* In earlier excavations on the site, some early Roman period storage pits and cisterns were also found.

Nazareth at the time of Jesus was a very small village settled by a few families. Nazareth was set in a small basin surrounded by hills and wasn't very accessible. It did have a water supply from what is called today Mary's Well, and there is evidence of some limited terraced agriculture, as well as pasture fields. But since the town wasn't located on a roadway, *"people didn't go through Nazareth unless they specifically wanted to go there"*.

While few remains of structures from the time of Jesus have been discovered, the most intriguing discoveries dating to the early Roman period is the proliferation of subterranean systems of rooms under ancient Nazareth that were hewn into the soft chalk bedrock.

The people who lived in Nazareth dug out pits for storage, and for other practical uses such as the production of wine, including treading grapes, and oil-pressing. Such storage pits have been found elsewhere in the Lower Galilee and Alexandre believes that the Jews eventually also used them for secreting their wares — aka tax evasion — and even themselves during the Great Revolt of 66 CE.

"What we did find in Nazareth is a development of this kind of concept — not only did they dig individual pits for storage, but they dug below the pits, down to a second level, deeper down, and a third level, and often there were underground passages leading from one to another. So really in the times of danger or in times when people wanted to hide things, they would be able to do so."

According to some experts, Nazareth in Jesus' day had a mixed population of gentiles and Jews.

Capernaum.

[The beginning of Jesus' public ministry]

Now when he heard that John had been arrested, he withdrew into Galilee and leaving Nazareth **he went and dwelt in Capernaum by the sea,** *in the territory of Zebulun and Naphtali, that what was spoken by the prophet Isaiah might be fulfilled:*
"The land of Zebulun and the land of Naphtali,
toward the sea, across the Jordan,
Galilee of the Gentiles—
the people who sat in darkness
have seen **a great light,**

and for those who sat in the region and shadow of death
light has dawned."
From that time Jesus began to preach, saying,
"Repent, for the kingdom of heaven is at hand."
[Matthew 4:13-17.]

Note: Zebulun and Naphtali were two Israelite tribes that were destroyed in the Assyrian invasion from 733 to 732 B.C

Extracts from Ritmeyer Archaeological Design website.
https://www.ritmeyer.com

Only Capernaum (which did not exist at the time of Isaiah) met the criteria in Isaiah's prophesy. Capernaum wraps around the northwest shore of the Sea of Galilee and was **located on Via Maris, the major trade route between Syria and Egypt.** Jesus' move from Nazareth to Capernaum was not a retreat into remoteness but a deliberate move into a more diverse region where his message and impact could have a wider and more receptive audience. It was nothing less than a move from the shadows to the spotlight. Capernaum was engaged with the world, via the International Highway and the Imperial Road.

This major highway was used by many traders, who, apart from buying and selling, also exchanged items of news. By living on the Via Maris, Jesus could be assured that what he did and said would be carried far and wide to the larger audience for whom his message was intended.

Excavations by Franciscan archaeologists have revealed that Capernaum was established in the 2nd century BC
Capernaum stretched for 300m along the shore and measured about 200m from north to south. The village was probably divided into four quarters with two sections of fishermen's

houses situated on either side of the southern part close to the sea and harbour, while wealthier houses, such as the ones belonging to the centurion, the ruler of the synagogue and the tax collector, were probably located closer to the hills.

The House of Peter where Jesus may have stayed was located between the synagogue and the harbour.

Peter's House
c. 30 AD
© Leen Ritmeyer

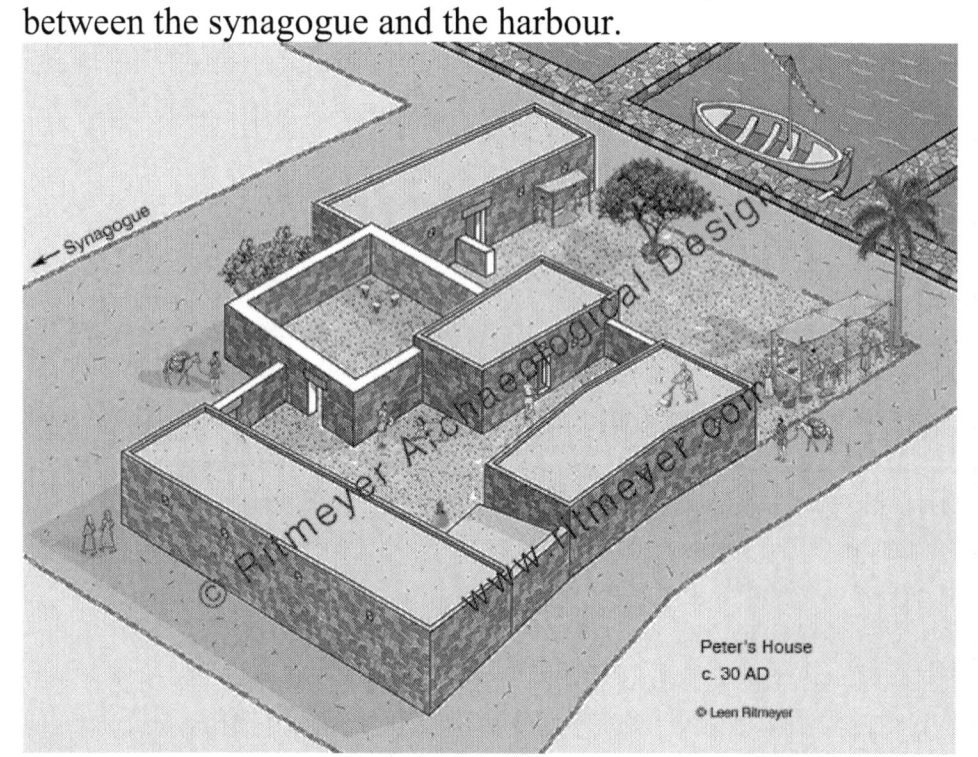

Peter's House consisted of ten rooms built around three courtyards. Most of the domestic activities took place in the northern courtyard. Animals were kept in the courtyard to the east, and the southern courtyard, which was next to the harbour, was presumably used for fishing activities such as mending nets, selling fish and other activities. Later in the century, the east courtyard was used as a place for religious gatherings.

Capernaum means the *Village of Comfort*. Jesus brought comfort to people that suffered from all sorts of diseases, to people that were politically and militarily oppressed by the

Romans, to people that wanted to hear the Gospel of the Kingdom of God, but received no spiritual comfort from their Jewish leaders. It was his home base.

Appendix:

Brief note of dates from Abraham to birth of Jesus.

[Note: there is still a great deal of debate among scholars about the exactitude of these dates.]

2,167 Birth of Abraham.
2,091 Calling of Abraham.
2,066 Isaac is born.
2,006 Jacob is born.
1,991 Death of Abraham.
1,915 Birth of Joseph.
1,886 Death of Isaac.

1,876 Jacob moves to Egypt.
1,859 Death of Jacob.
1,805 Death of Joseph.
1,800 Israel is in Egypt.

1,526 Birth of Moses.
1,486 Flight of Moses into the wilderness.
1,446 Moses is called by God.
------ The Exodus.
------ (Could be 200 years earlier!)
1,406 Entering the Promised Land.
------ Death of Moses.

1,400 The Promised Land conquered by Joshua.
1,043 The people reject God as their King. [1 Sam. 8:7]
------ Saul is appointed as king.
1,011 Death of Saul.
------ David becomes the king of Judah.
1,004 The kingdom is united.

971 Death of David.
---- Solomon is appointed as king.
931 Death of Solomon.
Many kings until
---- Ahaz reigns alone in Judah.

723 Israel is captured by the Assyrians.
716 Hezekiah is appointed king of Judah.
More kings until

586 The Babylonians take Judah into exile.

539 Persia overthrows Babylonia.
536 Beginning of the construction of the second Temple.
516 Completion of the Second Temple.

333 Alexander the Great rules over Palestine.
Ptolemies, Seleucids and Hasmoneans rule

63 Palestine is conquered by Rome.
37 Herod the Great is appointed as king.

The fullness of time.
4 Annunciation to the Virgin Mary.
4 Birth of John the Baptist.
4 Birth of Jesus.

For more: https://www.newadvent.org/cathen/03731a.htm

Appendix:

The structure of the Bible
As outlined in

St. Austin CATHOLIC Church & School
SERVED BY THE PAULIST FATHERS

Genesis 1 - 11 tells of the origins of the world and humanity before the advent of written history. These chapters are not intended as factual reporting of distinct, actual events. Whether or not these events happened as related in the Bible, they still speak to great truths in our understanding of who God is, and how we are called to relate to God. Genesis 12 - 50 relates the stories of the patriarchs Abraham, Isaac, Jacob, and Joseph, leaders in one family who related personally with God over four generations, c. 1800 - 1650 BC.

The Historical Books

The other four books of the Pentateuch are about events c. 1250 - 1200 BC. Jacob's descendants—called the Israelites—are numerous, but enslaved by the Pharoah in Egypt. God calls Moses to deliver the people from captivity. During the Red Sea's miraculous parting, the Israelites escape the Egyptians in a stunning reversal of fortunes. At Mt. Sinai, God gives the Israelites the Law (or Torah)—a covenant that they will follow in response to God protecting them—but the Israelites soon question God's commands. In response, God forces the Israelites to wander the desert for 40 years until the faithless generation has died out and been replaced.

Joshua leads the Israelites in a conquest of the Land of Canaan, the land originally promised by God to Abraham 600 years beforehand. But not all is peaceful. Other peoples still live in the land, and the Israelites sometimes give in to worshiping the gods of these other peoples.

Occasionally, God raises up a "judge"—a person who is both a prophet and a military leader—to bring the Israelites back to worship of God and defend the people from military attacks.

Samuel is the last of the judges. He anoints Saul as the first king of Israel. After Saul's death, David is anointed as the second king. He unites the entire nation of Israel c. 1000 and conquers the other peoples in the land. His son, Solomon, rules after him, taking the kingdom to its highest peak of peace and prosperity. Solomon builds the magnificent temple to house the ark of the covenant.

At the death of Solomon c. 930, the unified kingdom is divided by civil war. The northern kingdom, called Israel, Samaria, or Ephraim, is led by corrupt kings. Starting with Elijah, prophets rise up to condemn the kings. The northern kingdom is destroyed by the Assyrian Empire in 722, and ten tribes of the Israelites are dispersed by the Assyrians throughout the empire, losing their identity as a people.

David and Solomon's descendants rule the southern kingdom of Judah, which contains Jerusalem. It is led by some devout kings and some evil kings. Prophets advise and condemn these kings, too. After a string of corrupt kings after the death of King Josiah, the Babylonian Empire conquers the kingdom. The Judahite priests and aristocrats are taken away in exile to Babylon in 597, and the Babylonians destroy Jerusalem and its temple in 586.

The Babylonian exile is the greatest crisis of the Old Testament, forcing the religion to wrestle with how God could allow such a tragedy to befall the chosen people. It is during this time (586 - 538) that the religion of the "faithful remnant" of the descendants of Abraham is first called *Judaism* (the religion of the people of Judah). When Persia defeats Babylon in 539, King Cyrus allows the Judahites to return to rebuild the city and the temple. The second temple is dedicated in 515.

The next few centuries are not reported in many historical accounts, in the Bible or anywhere else. Judah, the vassal state that pays tribute to Persia, is conquered by the Macedonian Empire in 332 and is now called Judea (Greek name). Upon Alexander the Great's death in 323, Macdeonia breaks up into rival empires.

The Ptolemies, tolerant of Judaism like the Macedonians before them, rule 301 - 200. The Seleucids wrest control of Judea from the Ptolemies. The Seleucid rulers, especially Antichous IV, are intolerant of Judaism. Judas Maccabeus leads a revolt against the Seleucids, 167 - 164.

By 110, the new Hasmonean kingdom, led by Judas' family, is truly independent. Pompey of Rome conquers Judea in 63. Herod convinces the Romans to make him King of Judaea (Roman name) in 37.

The books of the Prophets.

While many of us might automatically associate "prophets" with future-telling and special acts of power, this does not represent the primary role of prophets in the Jewish and Christian traditions. Rather, a prophet is simply one who speaks God's truth on God's behalf. Jews traditionally recognize 55 prophets in the Old Testament, starting with Abraham and Sarah. While Christians do not typically categorize all 55 of these figures as prophets, we recognize some of them—even those who lived before the time of the divided kingdoms, including Moses, Samuel, and Nathan—as prophets.

The prophetic tradition reaches its full flowering in the northern kingdom of Israel starting c. 865 with Elijah and Elisha, whose deeds are recorded in 1 & 2 Kings. Other prophets of the northern kingdom are Amos and Hosea. Prophets of the southern kingdom (before the Babylonian exile) include Isaiah, Micah, Nahum, Habakkuk, Zephaniah, and Jeremiah.

Prophets during the exile include Ezekiel and perhaps Obadiah.

Prophets after the exile include Haggai, Zechariah, Baruch, Malachi, and Joel. The age of prophecy comes to a close with Joel c. 400.

Christianity traditionally categorizes 18 books as prophetic books, but we suggest categorizing 3 of them differently. Lamentations is a book of wisdom poetry grieving the destruction of Jerusalem in 586. Daniel is apocalyptic literature. Jonah is a fable of wisdom.

We traditionally break the prophetic books into the "major prophets" and the "minor prophets." The 6 major prophets are listed first—Isaiah, Jeremiah, Ezekiel, and Daniel because they are the longest books, and Lamentations and Baruch for their association with the prophet Jeremiah. The 12 minor prophets are shorter books that were traditionally written on a single scroll.

New Testament: The Gospels

For Christians, the gospels are by far the most important books of the Bible. They each detail the life, teaching, death, and resurrection of our Lord and Savior Jesus Christ. For those just beginning their study of the Bible, we recommend starting with the shortest Gospel, Mark, before moving on to Matthew, Luke, and John.

- *Matthew*
- *Mark*
- *Luke*
- *John*

The Acts of the Apostles is the second volume of a 2-part history of Christianity written in connection with the Gospel of Luke. Acts records the beginning of the Church at Pentecost, c. 30 AD, and how the gospel was then spread throughout the world by the nascent Church—guided by the Holy Spirit—in the next few decades, through c. 60. The main protagonists are the apostles Peter and Paul. Minor protagonists include the apostle John, the deacons Stephen and Philip, and the Christian leaders Barnabas and James, called "the brother of the Lord."

New Testament: The Epistles

Early leaders wrote a number of letters, or epistles, to Christian communities and individuals around the Roman Empire. 21 have been collected in the Bible.

The first 13 epistles in the Bible have traditionally been attributed to Paul. Hebrews is a treatise, written by an unknown disciple. The last seven epistles, written by authors other than Paul, are called the "catholic" letters because most of them are addressed to a more universal (i.e. catholic) audience.

New Testament: The Book of Revelation

Like the Book of Daniel in the Old Testament, the Book of Revelation is apocalyptic literature. Apocalyptic arose during Judeo-Christian religious persecutions c. 300 BC - 200 AD. It presents events of the present and the recent past in a new spiritual light—an unveiling or a revealing of new truths about God's plans that could not be grasped before.

The Book of Revelation was written at the end of the 1st century AD to Christians in Asia Minor undergoing extensive persecution by the Roman Empire. By symbolically presenting events of the recent past as if they were occurring as part of God's final cosmic victory over evil, the author of Revelation encourages the churches of Asia Minor to persevere.

Printed in Great Britain
by Amazon